PAUL TODD

DO YOU *REALLY* KNOW THE CHURCH?

ALBA BOOKS

ISBN — 0 — 8189 — 1140 — 9

Nihil Obstat:
  Rev. John J. Jennings
  Censor
  June 17, 1976

Imprimatur:
  + Most Rev. Daniel E. Pilarczk, D.D.
  Auxiliary Bishop of Cincinnati
  June 21, 1976

Library of Congress Catalog Card Number 76 – 27402
ISBN 0-8189-1140-9

© Copyright, 1977, by Alba House Communications
  Canfield, Ohio 44406

Printed in the United States of America

DO YOU *REALLY* KNOW THE CHURCH?

True ecumenism requires plain speaking and this is now almost a lost art. If we are to find our way out of the current confusion and return to sanity and sanctity we will simply have to stop telling people we don't know the answers. The fact is that we DO know the answers — but are afraid to give them.

There has been too much loose thinking followed by loose living. It is time Catholics resumed the time-honored practice of giving straight replies to straight questions.

You will find such questions and replies in this informative book.

DEDICATION

To Rev. Anthony Wolf, my former pastor and dear friend, for his spiritual direction, example and inspiration, this book is lovingly dedicated.

The Author

MR. PAUL TODD, through his professional work, came into contact with people in all walks of life and early realized that most Protestants have an incorrect idea about the Church and its teaching and — to our shame it must be said — rarely ask questions, because their Catholic friends are not likely to have satisfying answers.

In his spare time he became a freelance writer on religious issues and his column in several newspapers drew a favorable response.

He is now publishing an updated selection from this material in book form hoping that a wider circle of readers will learn facts rather than fantasy about the Church and that Church members will equally profit from this brief refresher course in the essentials.

Mr. Todd, who makes his home in Russells Point, Ohio, is also a former member of the Legion of Mary, a zealous Mission helper and a gifted organist.

CONTENTS

INTRODUCTION xi

THERE *IS* A GOD! 1

GOD HAS A MOTHER! 7
   Why honor Mary? 9
   Is she really God's Mother? 11
   Can we think too much of her? 13
   Why pray to Mary? 14
   Was she really a virgin? 15
   Her Immaculate Conception 17
   Her Assumption 19

THE CATHOLIC CHURCH 21
   The Bible is silent 23
   Only one rule of faith? 25
   Some other Churches 26
   The true Church 27
   Catholicism and Protestantism 28

POINTS OF CATHOLIC TEACHING 43
- The Eucharist 45
- The Mass 47
- Confessing Sins 48
- Priests forgive sins 50
- Attending Mass 51
- Catholic Ceremonies 52
- Images and Statues 54
- Indulgences 55
- Catholics and Masons 56
- Bible 57

POINTS OF CATHOLIC MORALITY 63
- Birth control 65
- Abortion 66
- Some Little-Known facts 69
- Vasectomy 71
- Homosexuality 71
- Euthanasia 74
- Divorce 77

OTHER QUESTIONS 79
- Aid for Parochial Schools 81
- The Pope is Peter 83
- Infallibility 84
- Purgatory 85
- Wealth of the Church 86
- Those "chained" Bibles 87
- Those "forbidden" Bibles 88
- The "bad Catholics" 89

AND NOW ... WHAT WILL YOU DO? 91
- On becoming a Catholic 93

INTRODUCTION

The purpose of this book is to enlighten those who believe wrong things about the Catholic Church. It is not to prove that you are "wrong"; it is not to prove that we are "right", it is merely to present the factual truth in order that the truth may conquer through the grace of God. My primary task is not to humble the erroneous; not to glorify the Catholic Church as intellectual and self-righteous, but to present the truth in a calm, clear manner. It is hoped that this book will show you that the Catholic Church is the only Church existing today which goes back to the time of Christ. History is so very clear on this point, it is curious how many minds miss its obviousness.

Minds cannot forever search in vain for religious truth; they must find something solid to fasten on, else die of spiritual anemia. To you, dear Protestant, this book may seem blunt and even shocking from your point of view. But believe this, no offense is intended. By the questions and answers in this book, I will point out undeniable facts which have been challenged by some of the greatest Protestant intellectuals since the sixteenth century, the period of the Reformation. But no one has ever been able to disprove the Church's claims.

We know that there are and that there have been millions and millions of good and devout Protestants. We are not callous to the spirituality and piety of our Protestant Brothers in Christ. But you are not being fair to yourself if you have not examined or don't propose to examine the case of the Catholic Church, and that from reliable sources. After all, any system that can claim the loyalty of 700,000,000 people is worth serious study, especially a system which such a long and unbroken tradition behind it.

There is a duty resting upon everyone to search for the truth, and thus to enlighten his conscience so that it will honestly reflect objective realities. I ask one favor of the Protestant reader: that he will examine the evidence presented in this book with an open mind.

Whether we realize it or not, personal responsibility to cooperate with divine grace, grows in proportion as we learn the depths and the practical bearings of Christian faith on dedicated Christian living. As to Catholicism, oldest of Churches and established by Christ, one has the full responsibility for full, complete investigation and an honest decision.

I sincerely feel, that reading this book will eliminate most of the intellectual confusion that has kept you in a long "state of search" and help you go straight for the essentials. The starkness of the age demands it. PRAY FOR A COURAGEOUS LOVE OF TRUTH.

I really don't believe that there are many people who actually hate the Catholic Church. There are millions, however, who are perplexed by what they wrongly believe to be the Catholic Church — which is, of course, quite a different thing. These millions can hardly be censured for blaming Catholics because Catholics "adore statues"; because they "put Mary on the same level with God"; because the Pope "is a Fascist"; because the "Church is the defender of Capitalism."

If the Church taught or believed any of these things it should be blamed, but the fact is that the Church does

Introduction

not believe nor teach them. As a matter of fact, if we Catholics believed all of the untruths and lies which have been said against the Church, we probably would be more upset with the Church than are Protestants. There is need for instruction if one is sincerely interested in seeking the truth. This modest volume aims at presenting some basic facts.

I have read this book, Do You Really Know the Church and find that it has much merit, sound in substance and readable in form. There is so little apologetic material of this kind today that this book should be welcome to many.

Most Rev. Leo A. Pursley, DD

Bishop of Fort Wayne-South Bend

THERE *IS* A GOD!

The Church holds that the recognition of God is in no way hostile to man's dignity, since this dignity is rooted and perfected in God... She further teaches that a hope related to the end of time does not diminish the importance of intervening duties... By contrast, when a divine substructure and the hope of eternal life are wanting, man's dignity is most grievously lacerated... The riddles of life and death, of guilt and of grief go unsolved, with the frequent result that men succumb to despair.

Second Vatican Council: *The Church Today*

There is a God!

What makes you so sure that there is a God? I am an Atheist and have never heard any facts that could convince me that there is a Supreme Being.

As I understand it, your profession of atheism represents the denial of the existence of God. In theory, you make your own judgment that there is no God. You doubt either the existence of God as not sufficiently proved or you consider every clear statement about God to be impossible because it exceeds your finite knowledge, understanding and most of all, your sincerity in reasoning logically.

You regard recognition of dependence on God as incompatible with human freedom and independence. Another position you hold to is the belief that God sedates man on earth, reconciling him to acceptance of suffering, injustice and shortcomings, because of hope for greater things after death.

Now if you think that in order to convince you that evidence of the existence of God must be seen or heard, such as a thundering voice from the sky saying "I AM GOD", or a large image of Him flashed on the clouds, of course we cannot prove it that way. No reasonable person would expect such a display of Deity just to satisfy some egocentric mortal human of His existence. God certainly does not have to prove Himself to non-believers.

But, let's see if we can find sufficient scientific evidence to satisfy you that there must be a Supreme Being. First of all let us explore the basic principles of physics and causality.

Causality is the formulated regularity with which an effect depends on its cause, or the cause brings forth its effect. The universe limited in all its details, could not be its own cause. It could no more come into existence with all its regulating laws than a clock could assemble itself and keep perfect time without a clock maker.

No mere chance can produce order, so there must be a Planner, who is God. We know that certain laws of nature exist so there must be a Law Giver, who is God. Dependent, contingent, unnecessary beings exist, so there must be an Independent Necessary Being, who is God. All effects have causes so there must be a First Cause, who is God. Of course for the acceptance of these arguments it is necessary that you accept the truths that are self-evident: your reason and your senses.

Look up into the great vast sky at the Master Clock of the universe, which according to our most eminent scientists is at least four billion years old, which never misses a second, the perfect watch by which you must constantly set all imperfect man-made watches and clocks. Can you tell me that "It all just happened"? That there was no great Watchmaker? That no Mastermind thought out and planned our vast universe, brought it into being, set each star and planet in its own exact place and started the heavenly bodies coursing through space each in its prescribed orbit, in its orderly precision? Can you say that it just fashioned itself, put itself together, wound itself up and started itself running?

Has it possibly ever occurred to you that you could be wrong? I believe that your fear that there might be a

There is a God!

God may be perhaps unconscious. There is a strong possibility that you deny that God exists in order to be free in your own mind of moral obligations. Even if this is so, even if you deny God, be certain that God will never deny you! If you are reading these lines now, it is because He wants you to read them. But they are only the beginning. Read and study more. Be honest with yourself ... and see what happens!

GOD HAS A MOTHER

At the message of the angel, the Virgin Mary received the Word of God in her heart and in her body, and gave Life to the world. Hence she is acknowledged and honored as being truly the Mother of God and Mother of the Redeemer. Redeemed in an especially sublime manner by reason of the merits of her Son, and united to Him by a close and indissoluble tie, she is endowed with the supreme office and dignity of being the Mother of the Son of God ... At the same time, however, because she belongs to the offspring of Adam, she is one with all human beings in their need for salvation.

Second Vatican Council: *The Church*

WHY HONOR MARY?

Why do Catholics pay so much honor to Mary, when she was only an ordinary woman?

The Catholic Church has always paid special honor to Mary, because God the Father honored her above all creatures by bestowing upon her the highest dignity He could confer, the divine maternity. God the Son honored her by choosing her for His own dear mother and by bestowing affection and unsurpassable dignity upon her. God the Holy Spirit honored her by taking her for His special spouse, and by miraculously causing Jesus to be conceived in her womb.

We honor our heroes and statesmen without detracting from the honor we owe to God. We erect monuments and statues to our fellowmen as an inspiration to patriotism. We make national shrines of the birthplace of our heroes. Shall we then be reproached if we honor and erect shrines to her who is the greatest woman who ever lived, a woman whom Almighty God Himself so singularly blessed and to whom He assigned the most glorious mission ever committed to a mortal?

Your attention is directed to the prophecy of God Himself to the serpent (devil) *"I will put enmities between thee and the woman, and thy seed and her seed;*

she shall crush thy head, thou shalt lie in wait for her heel". (Gen. 3; 15) Such was the devotion to Mary which the early Christians bequeathed to the Church. Would we not be traitors to our heritage, were we to minimize or deny the honor due to her whom God, the Father honored in the very creating of her soul?

Are we mere creatures of God, to have less respect and love for His choice as a mother by being critical of what seems like extravagance of devotion, or is due to misunderstanding? Surely, dear reader, I do not include you in this category, or you would not have taken the time or trouble to read this about Mary.

Perhaps you are wondering why God did not reveal these things more clearly through the Holy Scriptures. He did not reveal these mysteries in the primitive Church because they are so great that the faithful would have been lost in the contemplation and admiration of them at the time when it was necessary to establish firmly the law of grace and of the Gospel. Although all mysteries of religion are in perfect harmony with each other, yet human ignorance might have suffered recoil and doubt at their magnitude, when faith in the Incarnation and Redemption and the precepts of the new law of the Gospel were yet in their beginnings. On this same account, Jesus said to His disciples at the Last Supper: *"Many things have I to say to you, but you are not yet disposed to receive them".* (John 16, 30) These words He addressed to all the world, for it was not yet capable of giving full obedience to the law of grace and full assent to the Faith in the Son; much less was it prepared to be introduced into the mysteries of His Mother.

IS SHE REALLY GOD'S MOTHER?

Why do Catholics call Mary the Mother of God?

Sometimes we Catholics take our Protestant friends

God Has a Mother! 11

and neighbors too much for granted, by not realizing that too often we use terminologies in our faith that they do not understand, which have little meaning and even appear blasphemous to them. Today there are many terms used by Protestants and Catholics alike which are not found in the Bible, such as Trinity, Incarnation; yet every genuine Protestant believes in the truths in these terms. Thus it is the truth we look to find in the Bible, and not necessarily the present day terminology of it.

The Angel pointed out that Mary's child would be called the Son of God. *"And the angel answering said to her: 'The Holy Ghost shall come upon thee, and the power of the most High shall overshadow thee. And therefore also the Holy which shall be born of thee shall be called the Son of God'."* — (Luke 1; 35) And Jesus put forth that very claim, namely to be the Son of God and equal to the Father. *"Hereupon therefore the Jews sought the more to kill him, because he did not only break the sabbath, but also said God was His Father, making Himself equal to God. Then Jesus answered, and said to them: Amen, amen, I say unto you, the Son cannot do anything of Himself, but what He seeth the Father doing; for what things soever he doth, these the Son doth in like manner. For the Father loveth the Son, and sheweth Him all things which Himself doth; and greater works than these will He shew Him, that you may wonder. For as the Father raiseth up the dead, and giveth life to whom He will, so the Son grants life to whom He wishet. For neither doth the Father judge any man, but hath given judgment to the Son. That all men may honor the Son, as they honor the Father.* (John 5; 18-23)

He proved this statement by miracles. Now, Mary is the Mother of Jesus, and she is the Mother of the Son of God. But the Son of God is God. So, Mary is the Mother of God.

Thomas said to Jesus after he put his hand in his side where the lance had pierced: *"My Lord and my God".*

(John 20; 28) If Jesus was not God, He certainly would have rebuked Thomas for these words. It was revealed by the Holy Spirit to Elizabeth that Mary's child was the Lord. Elizabeth cried out: *"And how have I derserved that the Mother of my Lord should come to me"*. (Luke 1; 43) Lord and God, the person is the same.

The key to understanding Mary is this: we do not start with Mary. We start with Christ, the Son of the Living God. The more we think of Him, the more we think of her; the more we adore His Divinity, the more we venerate her motherhood. It is on account of Our Divine Lord that Mary receives special attention, and not on account of herself. Left to herself, His mother would dissolve into ordinary motherhood. But when seen in the light of His Divinity, she becomes unique. Our Lord is God who became man. Never before or since did Eternity become Time in a woman, nor did Omnipotence take on the bonds of flesh in a maid. It is her Son who makes her motherhood different.

Is it any wonder then that we love to pay honor to the Mother of God? For all these different forms of tribute which Catholics heap upon Mary, we have the sanctions of Holy Writ and the support of the traditions of countless generations. Through twenty long centuries the Catholic Church has unceasingly paid a large amount of honor to Mary and thereby fulfilled the prophecy: *"All generations shall call me blessed"*. (Luke 1; 48) Heaven has thus taken the lead in honoring Mary. No man can give her higher honors than those God has given her.

CAN WE THINK TOO MUCH OF HER?

When you Catholics honor Mary, doesn't that alone detract from the honor that is due to Jesus?

Mary does not prevent our honoring Our Lord. Noth-

God Has a Mother!

ing is more cruel than to say that she takes souls away from Christ. That could mean that Our Lord chose a mother who is selfish, He, who is Love itself. If she kept us from her Son, we would disown her. We would never have had Our Divine Lord if He had not chosen her.

If her Divine Son had not intended that His mother should be honored where He is adored, He would never have permitted these prophetic words to have had fulfillment. The angel's salutation was, *"Hail, full of grace, the Lord is with thee: Blessed art thou among women".* (Luke 1; 28) Elizabeth, her cousin was filled with the Holy Spirit and cried out, *"Blessed art thou among women and blessed is the fruit of thy womb".* (Luke 1: 42) Then Mary answered Elizabeth in the beautiful Magnificat, *"Henceforth all generations shall call me blessed".* (Luke 1; 48) That is why Catholics call her "Our blessed Mother" and the "Blessed Virgin".

There is never any danger that men will think too much of Mary. The danger is that they will think too little of Christ. Coldness toward Mary is a consequence of the indifference to Christ. Any objection to calling her the "Mother of God" is fundamentally an objection to the Deity of Christ. If I would come to your home to visit you and coldly ignored your mother, I'm sure your feeling toward me would be anything but warm, wouldn't it? Don't you think that Jesus would feel hurt too if you came before Him, told how much you loved Him, while at the same time you coldly ignored His heavenly Mother?

WHY PRAY TO MARY?

I. Tim. II, 5 says that there is one mediator between God and man, the man Christ Jesus.

Correct, and Catholics also believe that.

Then why do Catholics pray to the Virgin Mary and other saints to make intercession for them?

First of all, because praying to the Blessed Virgin and the saints is not opposed to the passage you quote. Catholics believe that Jesus Christ alone redeemed us by His death upon the cross, thus reconciling us to God, and making us partakers of His grace here and His glory hereafter. No divine gift can reach us except through Christ and the merits of His sacred passion. Therefore, every prayer we pray, and every prayer in heaven of the Blessed Virgin, and the saints, have their efficacy only through Jesus Christ our Lord. The Blessed Virgin and the saints simply add their prayers to ours, and, although specially pleasing to God because of their greater holiness, they aid us only though the merits of the one mediator, Jesus Christ.

Without the sacrifice of Christ, the human race would never have been redeemed. No other prayers and sacrifices could have brought this about. But the Mediator Himself can be surrounded with other helpers or mediators as is clear from the vision in Revelation 5, 8 where the twenty-four elders "have in their hands golden bowls of incense, which are the prayers of the saints".

Mary united her prayers with those of her Son throughout the entire life of Jesus: at the crib, in Egypt, in Nazareth, during His public life, and under the Cross. What could have been closer to the Heart of Mary than the salvation of souls? In this sense she is truly mediating together with her Son for the salvation of men. No Catholic thinks of her as mediating apart or independently of her Son. In fact, we all are mediators when we pray for one another.

Concentrating on the fact that Christ is the one principal Mediator, have you made any allowance for the equally clear doctrine of secondary mediation of one human being for another with, in, and through Christ? Most Protestants repeat the words of the Apostles Creed, "I believe in the Communion of Saints". It has always been my belief that these good people understood it as we do. We understand this doctrine and know that member can help member. We accept the teaching of St. James, "that the prayer of a just soul availeth much". And first and foremost among the just is the Mother of Christ. She is with God; she is interested in all whom Jesus died to redeem; can the Son repulse His own mother? Undoubtedly not.

WAS SHE REALLY A VIRGIN?

I am a Bible scholar, so don't try to hand me anything that you can't prove from the Bible. How can you say that Mary, the mother of Jesus, remained a virgin when the Bible expressly speaks of the brethren of the Lord, James, Joseph, Simon and Jude?

I will never cease to be mystified by the Bible scholars and even some clergymen who still hold to the idea that Mary had other children after Jesus was born. If they will only read on a little further, the Bible will explain itself. It is true that the Bible refers to the "brethren" of Jesus, but the Aramaic word means "cousins", although it was translated into Hebrew as "brethren".

When reading the Bible, we discover that not only those born of the same mother are called brother, but also cousins, nephews and even more distant relations. Innumerable instances in the Old Testament prove this; e.g. "brother" is used in Genesis for nephews, in Leviticus for distant cousins, in I Paralipomenon for first cousins and in Job for relatives in general. Lot is called Abraham's brother, whereas he was Abraham's nephew (*Gen. 14; 12 & 14; 16*) Jacob called Leban his brother whereas he was both cousin and nephew to him. (*Gen. 29; 10 & 29; 12*).

Since these are all possible meanings for the Hebrew word "brothers", absolutely nothing can be proven from its use in connection with Jesus. Moreover, what evidence we have of the families of the men whom you claim to be the "brothers of Jesus" shows that James, Joseph, Simon and Jude were actually cousins of Jesus. Their father was Cleophas, sometimes he was called Alpheus.

In the next few texts, if you will study the references diligently, you will see what I mean. There were only two men by the name of "James" mentioned in the Bible. One was the son of Zebedee and the other was the son of Alpheus. The later James is the one that you claim to be the "brother of the Lord." *And the names of the twelve apostles are these: The first, Simon who is called Peter, and Andrew his brother. James the son of Zebedee and John his brother, Philip and Bartholomew, Thomas and Matthew the publican, and JAMES THE SON OF ALPHEUS, and Thaddeus, Simon the Cananean, and Judas Iscariot, who also betrayed Him.* (Matt. 10; 2-3-4)

Among whom was Magdalen, and Mary the mother of James and Joseph, and the mother of the sons of Zebedee. (Matt. 27; 56)

And Mary Magdalen, and Mary the mother of Joseph, beheld where He was laid. (Mark 15; 47)

And when the sabbath was past, Mary Magdalen, and Mary the mother of James, and Salome, bought sweet spices, that coming, they might anoint Jesus. (Mark 16; 1)

And it was Mary Magdalen, and Joanna, and Mary the mother of James, and the other women that were with them, who told these things to the apostles. (Luke 24: 10)

Jude, the servant of Jesus Christ, and brother of James: to them that are beloved in God the Father, and preserved in Jesus Christ, and called. (Jude 1; 1)

Now there stood by the cross of Jesus, His mother; and His mother's sister, Mary of Cleophas, and Mary Magdalen. When Jesus therefore had seen His mother and the disciple standing whom He loved, He saith to His mother: Woman, behold thy son. After that, he saith to

God Has a Mother! 17

the disciple: Behold thy mother. And from that hour, the disciple took her to his own. (John 19; 25; 26; 27)

Now, just stop and think. Do you actually believe that Our Lord, while He was dying on the cross, would have commended His mother to the care of John, the beloved disciple, had He blood brothers, as you claim? Unless Mary were resolved to remain a virgin, why would she have said to the angel at the Annunication, "How shall this happen, since I do not know man?" Her surprise and wonder would have had no meaning because she was engaged to Joseph and ready to begin living with him. If she had later broken the resolution here implied and had other children, why would St. Luke have recorded her words, "How shall this happen since I do not know man?"

HER IMMACULATE CONCEPTION

What do you mean by the Immaculate Conception, that is in connection with Mary.

The Immaculate Conception does not mean that Mary was conceived miraculously, or that there was anything abnormal in her physical origin. It simply means that her soul was preserved from that taint of original sin which all others inherit from their first parents. It was really an anticipated baptism, a redemption of Mary's soul by prevention of sin's contamination and through the merits of Christ.

I always thought that the Immaculate Conception was the virgin birth of Christ. Now you say that the Immaculate Conception pertains to Mary, His mother.

Yes, I'm afraid you are confused by these two separate doctrines. The Immaculate Conception is a term referring to the conception of Mary herself by her parents, Joachim and Anne. When Mary was conceived, her soul was preserved immaculate, or free from inherited original sin. But when Mary herself conceived Jesus, it was under the influence of the Holy Spirit, and not through any relations with man.

Usually it is referred to as the Virgin Birth, since it implies that Jesus was born of a virgin. That Jesus was born of a virgin mother has been explicitly taught by the Catholic Church from the beginning. So in the Apostles' Creed itself we say, "born of the Virgin Mary." That the doctrine of the Immaculate Conception of Mary herself is also part of the Christian revelation was defined by the Church in 1854. The Church did not invent a new doctrine then. She merely defined that such was the original Christian teaching of the New Testament.

Why do you claim that the Virgin Mary never committed sin, when the Bible says: "If we say that we have no sin, we deceive ourselves, and the truth is not in us" (John I, 8)

Is it not reasonable to suppose that our Blessed Lord, by the bestowal of special graces, would preserve His own Mother from the smallest sin? Let's put it this way: Jesus was carried in His Mother's womb for nine months: the greatest privilege ever given to a woman. Her body was the Tabernacle of the Most High, the temporary abode of the Son of God. Since sin is always associated with the devil in one form or another, it would be most unreasonable to think, or believe that God the Father, and the Holy Spirit, would allow Jesus to be carried in the womb of a woman, who had the slightest stain of sin.

HER ASSUMPTION

Please explain fully the Assumption of the Blessed Virgin Mary.

The doctrine says that, after her life on earth ended her

body was spiritualized and glorified; at once being assumed into heaven. In other words, God anticipated for the Blessed Virgin Mary what is going to happen to all the saved on the last day.

What reasons are there for her bodily assumption?

Mary, by her Immaculate Conception, was preserved free from all taint of original sin. She shared in the whole work of redemption, identifying herself with Jesus in all His sorrows and sufferings. And, as she shared in His redemptive work, so also she shared in the privilege of His resurrection and glory. After all, it was just as easy for God to take her glorified body to heaven at once as it will be to take the glorified bodies of all the saved.

But there is nothing in Scripture about the Assumption of Mary into Heaven. What authority is there for this doctrine?

The Catholic Church teaches the Assumption of the Blessed Virigin Mary into heaven. But what reasons support the teaching?

There is no express reference to the subject in Sacred Scripture. But it has been the tradition of Christians from the very beginning. The conviction of the fact did not arise from mere belief; the belief can only be accounted for by the primitive fact.

The Greek Orthodox Church agrees with the Catholic Church on this doctrine. The High Church Anglicans are returning to it. I have just been reading an Anglican booklet on the subject, in which the author writes: "It would seem rash to deny such a bodily Assumption, for despite the prevalence of credulity in the matter of relics, no Church, or city has ever claimed to possess the mortal remains of our Lady."

Why not? It is a fact that requires explanation. Relics of our Lady would possess a great value for Christians. St.

Peter's bones, for example, are reverenced at Rome. but no city has ever claimed to possess the remains of our Blessed Lady. Her assumption, body and soul, into heaven is one good reason why.

THE CATHOLIC CHURCH

This is the unique Church of Christ which in the Creed we avow as one, holy, catholic and apostolic. After His Resurrection our Savior handed her over to Peter to be shepherded (Jn. 21: 17), commissioning him and the other apostles to propagate and govern her (Mt. 28: 18 ff.) ... This Church, constituted and organized in the world as a society, subsists in the Catholic Church which is governed by the successor of Peter and by the bishops in union with that successor...

Second Vatican Council: *The Church*

THE BIBLE IS SILENT

How can you claim the Catholic Church is the only existing Church today which goes back to the time of Christ? The Catholic Church is not once mentioned in the Bible.

First of all let's make sure that we both understand what the word "Catholic" means. The word "Catholic" means "Universal". Applied to the Church it means one and the same Church found everywhere in the world, believing the same truths, teaching men of all nations exactly the same religion and uniting them under one and the same authority.

The word "Catholic" was first applied to the Church by St. Ignatius, Bishop of Antioch, who died in the year 107 A.D. He used the word to describe the universality of the Church founded by Christ and subject to the Bishop of Rome. It was in the year 325 A.D. at the Council of Nicaea that the word "Catholic" was adopted formally.

It is true that the world "Catholic" is not found in the Bible. It is not a question of a *name* but of a *thing*. The universal spiritual society now known as "the Catholic Church" is most clearly described in Scripture. Christ said clearly that His Church would be one fold under one shepherd, the fold embracing all nations, the shepherd being St. Peter and his successors. Either the Catholic Church is the one Christ established, or His Church has altogether ceased to exist.

Most Protestants believe in the Trinity, but the word "Trinity" cannot be found in the Bible either! There are several other terms they use and firmly believe, yet they are not in the Bible.

Actually, we read in 2-Peter, 1-20, "No Scripture is of private interpretation". The ideal that each man has a right to his own private interpretation of Scripture is anti-Scriptural. *St. Peter warns against private interpretation in Verse 20, giving the reasons in Verse 21.* The sense is as follows: "Do not presume to think you may privately interpret Scripture for yourself. If Scripture were merely the result of natural human thought, it would be different. But it is not merely human thought. The holy writers were inspired by God and it is the Spirit of God, not your own reasoning, which can dictate the true sense." *In the same Epistle, 111, 16, St. Peter obviously shows that he was opposed to private interpretation when he says that there are many things in the Scripture hard to understand and which the unlearned and unstable wrest to their own destruction.*

Let's put this same situation in another way. We do not trust the interpretation of the Constitution of the United States to an individual no matter how learned he may be. If a question as to its meaning arises, there is but one authoritative declaration and that is the Supreme Court. The Bible may be considered the Constitution of the world-wide Church. The Catholic Church, the Church that gave the Bible to the world, may in case of doubt declare truly the meaning of the Bible. In collecting the material of the Bible, she discriminates between the true and false.

ONLY ONE RULE OF FAITH?

We Protestants believe that the Bible is the only rule of faith and anything outside of that is not worth reading or listening to.

The Bible cannot be the sole rule of faith because the faithful are urged in the Epistles to believe all they learned from the preaching of the Apostles. *"Preach the Gospel to every creature," "Therefore Brethren"*, St. Paul writes, *"Stand fast and hold the traditions you have learned by word only or by our epistles."* (Thess. 2, 14) This is affirmed also by *St. John: "I had many things to write unto thee, but I would not by pen and ink write to thee, but I hope speedily to see thee: And we will speak face to face".* (3 John 13, 14).

Why did not Christ say: *"Write* the Gospel to all nations? " Why did not Christ write himself? Why did some write, but occasionally, and so late, and often to private individuals?

The Bible cannot be the sole rule of faith. Search the Scriptures and you will never find anywhere that they are the only rule of faith. Nowhere in the entire compass of the holy writings is there a text or passage either suggesting or enunciating the principle of the Bible alone.

Jesus Christ never said: "Go, sit ye down and write Bibles, scatter them about and tell every man to guess for himself." No, Christ sent forth His Apostles with the power to teach the nations of the earth. St. Matthew wrote his Gospel years after Christ had left the world. So for years the Church was in existence before we had even one written word of the New Testament. St. Mark also wrote after Christ's departure. So did St. Luke. St. John wrote between A.D. 90 and 100. So we find the Catholic religion in existence for up to sixty years before any Gospel was either written or collected, or completed! What of all the primitive Christians without the Bible to guide them during that time? Does that not indicate that the Bible is not now and never was the only rule of faith?

SOME OTHER CHURCHES

Can you please tell me the history of the Christian Religions and where does the Catholic Church fit in?

If you mean by your question, "when did the different religions start"? I respectfully submit these historical facts.

If you are a *Lutheran*, your religion was founded by Martin Luther, an ex-monk of the Catholic Church in the year 1517.

If you are a *Presbyterian*, your religion was founded by John Knox in Scotland in the year 1560.

If you are a *Methodist*, your religion was founded by John and Charles Wesley in England in the year 1744.

If you are a *Baptist*, your religion was founded by John Smyth who launched it in Amsterdam in the year 1606.

If you worship with the *Salvation Army*, your sect began with William Booth in London in 1865.

If you are a *Christian Scientist*, your religion was started by Mrs. Baker Eddy in the year 1879.

If you are a *Protestant Episcopalian*, your religion was an off-shoot of the Church of England, founded by Samuel Seabury in the American colonies in the 17th century.

If you belong to one of the religious organizations known as "Church of the Nazarene", "Pentecostal Gospel", "Holiness Church", "Pilgrim Holiness Church", Jehovah's Witnesses", your religion is one of the hundreds of new sects founded by men within the past sixty years.

If you are a *Roman Catholic*, you know that your religion was founded in the year 33 by Jesus Christ the Son of God, and that it has not changed since that time.

(The accuracy of these historical facts can be verified in any Encyclopedia.)

THE TRUE CHURCH

How can you be so sure that the Catholic Church is the true Church? If so, how can you prove it?

Did you examine the title deed of the lot on which your home stands? If you did, you discovered that the deed traces the title back to the original owner, the government of the United States. If it did not, the title would be worthless. An attorney has occasion to check the validity of the title deeds of his clients. In doing this he would go to the county records office and verify the fact that the deed traced the title back to the original owner.

If we require the title of property to be traced back to the original owner, the United States Government, why shouldn't we likewise require the title of the full deposit of religious truth to be traced back to the original owner, Jesus Christ? You may have been going along for years on the widespread assumption that one religion is as good as another and that all churches speak with equal authority. But can you reconcile the principle involved in such an assumption with the principle by which you determine the validity of a title to property?

The Lutheran Church was founded by Martin Luther in Germany in the year 1517. This means that Jesus Christ, the Founder of the Christian Religion and the first owner of the full deposit of revealed truth, had never heard of the Lutheran religion. He could not, therefore, have authorized, sanctioned, or commissioned the Lutheran Church to teach in His name. In other words, its title was defective. The gap of nearly 1500 years between the foundation of the Church of Christ and the establishment of the Lutheran Church by Martin Luther was so great that no careful investigator could fail to see the invalidity of its title deed.

If this is true of the title deed of the first Protestant Church, obviously it is also true of all other Protestant denominations. Now look at the title deed of the Catholic Church. Open the Bible and read for me the words spoken by Christ to Peter: *"Thou art Peter and upon this rock I will build My Church, and the gates of hell shall not prevail against it. And I will give to thee the keys to the kingdom of heaven". And whatsoever thou shalt bind upon earth, it shall be bound also in heaven: and whatsoever thou shalt loose on earth, it shall be loosed also in heaven".* (Matt. 16; 18; 19).

In these clear words, Christ conferred upon Peter, the chief of the Apostles and the head of His Church on earth, as well as upon Peter's successors, authority to teach His truths to all mankind. A list of all the Pontiffs, from Peter to the present Pope shows that there has been unbroken succession and that the Catholic Church is the only Church with a flawless "title deed" to prove her claims.

CATHOLICISM AND PROTESTANTISM

It seems to me that Protestantism and Catholicism are founded on the same basic principles, their differences being due to different interpretation of the Bible, is this not true?

They are not founded on the same basic principles. In basic principles they are diametrically opposed. The basic principle of Protestantism is belief in what one thinks the Bible to mean. One makes an act of faith in one's own judgment. The Catholic basic principle is very different. Instead of deciding for himself what is or is not the teaching of Christ, the Catholic is taught to rely on the teaching of the Church. He knows that his own judgment could quite likely be wrong, but that the Catholic Church cannot be wrong. This promise was made by Christ Himself over nineteen centuries ago.

The Catholic priest does not preach merely his own opinions. He knows that his Church is not a particular sect, but a vast united universal Apostolic Church, whose history shows its origin, beginning with Christ. And such a Church is impossible to account for by merely human forces. It is God's work on the very face of it.

The Catholic submits to the Church's authoritative teaching in matters of faith and morals, rather than decide for himself what the Bible must mean. As recorded at the end of the Gospel of St. Matthew, these are the very last words uttered by Christ before He ascended into heaven. *And Jesus coming, spoke to them, saying: All power is given to me in heaven and in earth. Going therefore, teach ye all nations; baptizing them in the name of the Father, and of the Son, and of the Holy Ghost. Teaching them to observe all things whatsoever I have commanded you: and behold I am with you all days, even to the consummation of the world.* (Matt. 28; 18; 19; 20)

That certainly doesn't mean that one is at liberty to "pick and choose". Christ never even hinted that we have a right to decide to take what we like and leave what we don't like. The hundreds of different denominations of Christianity can't all be teaching "all things whatsoever I have commanded you", or else there would be no difference among them.

"I am with you ALL days". You've never heard of a better guarantee than that. Never once does Christ force acceptance of His truth. He leaves each person free to accept or reject His teachings. On the other hand, never does He "water down the truth", compromise, or give the idea that anyone is free to believe "what he likes". He says, in effect, "take it or leave it, but don't forget the consequences".

What is your attitude towards the Protestant Church?

Protestantism is a name covering many different sects which agree in protesting against the claims of the Catholic Church. I might add that many doctrines are attributed to Rome which Rome has never taught. In this case, Protestants simply do not understand the religion they oppose. It must be noted, too, that Protestants are anything but agreed amongst themselves as to what should be condemned in Catholic teaching.

When did the Protestant Reformation begin?

In the sixteenth century. Luther, in Germany, broke away from the Catholic Church in 1517, and set up a new Church for himself. Henry VIII, in England, abandoned the Catholic Church in 1534, when he brought in the law of his supremacy over the Church in his own realm. It would take too long to narrate how each of the first Protestants broke away. In various ways, each rebelled against Church authority. Luther denied her teaching. Henry VIII defended her teachings, but violated her discipline.

What made the people abandon the Catholic faith?

There were three chief causes: Firstly, most of the people were not very well instructed in their religion, and were greatly disaffected towards the Catholic Church by the laxity of the clergy whose disedifying lives left the people ready to back up any preacher who seemed sincere, whether he was right or wrong in matters of doctrine.

Secondly, John Knox came from Geneva to preach straight-out Calvinism with zeal and energy.

Thirdly, John Knox had the armed support of the nobles who sought to possess themselves of Church property.

Will you please explain what you consider the main cause for the loss of so many people to the Church at the Reformation?

There was nothing wrong with the Catholic religion. But there were a good many things wrong with great numbers of Catholics, or the Reformation would have been impossible. No one single cause can explain it. The conduct of those who left the Church must be attributed firstly to their infidelity to the grace of God in their own personal lives, and to their own pride and passions. But that so many should follow these leaders demands explanation. Mass defections from the Church happen only in a given atmosphere. And, unfortunately, many factors were at hand to contribute to the disaster.

Political causes had weakened the authority of the Pope. The covetous and avaricious also saw the possibility of loot and plunder in the confiscation of Church property. So they supported the rebellion even by force of arms. Many of the bishops and priests, far removed from Rome, had been too subservient to secular authority, and had neglected to enforce the discipline of the Church, thus weakening their hold upon the people. Careless priests had left the faithful uninstructed, and incredibly ignorant of their religion. Not knowing their own faith, great numbers of simple Catholics did not recognize the real evil of the separatist movement. Not knowing the truth, they were swayed by the ideas of the Reformers, who denounced Rome without demanding any higher standard of virtue than that which had prevailed. When the temporal rulers backed up the campaign with violence and oppression, the people simply found themselves Protestants. There were many other factors, which a brief reply cannot describe.

In view of this, was not reform necessary?

Yes. But there was no need for what is popularly called "The Reformation." Any abuses amongst the members of the Church will always cry out urgently for reform. But Protestantism was not a movement of real reform. It made prevalent abuses an excuse to abandon the Church altogether, instead of remaining with it, and trying to effect the conversion of its lax members to better ways. Moreover, Protestantism retained many of the abuses, and merely sought to justify them by denying that they are wrong.

Would the Reformers have had any success had they been dealing with present-day Catholics?

Not with well-instructed and sincere Catholics who are genuinely trying to live up to their religion. The ignorant and careless would be quite likely to fall away, above all if a less-exacting religion were proposed to them, and if the civil power were employed on behalf of the would-be Reformers. Where good Catholics have made an heroic stand, and even died for their faith, careless Catholics have fallen away. History contains many useful lessons. The Church cannot fail. But its members can and do fail. And their greatest safeguards against failures are a thorough knowledge of their religion, and a life of virtue in accordance with its teachings. Sound education, integrity of character, and a genuine effort to live a life of Christian holiness, are necessary for the growth and well-being of the Church in whatever country it may be established.

Did not Martin Luther force the Church to reform herself?

The multitudes swept from the Church by Protestantism certainly brought home to her leaders the urgent need for reform. But that reform was effected by the Council of Trent. The severe legislation and disciplinary decrees of that Council eradicated the pronounced abuses which gave occasion to the Protestant landslide from the Church.

Surely, then the Church owes some thanks to Martin Luther?

Luther had no right to leave the Church, and commence a Church of his own under the pretense of reform. He should have remained in the true Church and labored to reform lax Catholics within it. You wash a plate that needs cleansing; you do not smash it.

Since Christ commanded men to carry on His work, were not men free to form new Churches if necessary?

The mere fact that men were ordered to carry on the work of Christ Himself shows that they were not free to form new Churches according to their own ideas. That would be their own work, not Christ's work. Delegates are free to act within the jurisdiction given them by their principals, not to go beyond it. St. Paul denied that he, Apostle though he was, had any right to form a new and different Church. "Though we," he wrote to the Galatians, "or an angel from heaven, preach a gospel differing from what you have received, let him be anathèma." Gal. 1; 8 And to the Corinthians he wrote, "Let there be no schisms amongst you." I Cor. 12; 25 If the Apostles themselves had no right to set up new independent Churches, they could not possibly have transmitted such a right to others.

Do you deny that the Reformers had any divine authority for their work?

I do. They had no divine authority to commence new forms of religion and they did so in opposition to the clear teaching of the New Testament. A *reform*, not a *repudiation* of the Church was needed. Our Lord said that His Church would be like a net holding good and bad fish. At the time of the Reformation there were altogether too many bad fish. But bad fish do not make a bad net. And instead of laboring to turn the bad fish into good ones, the Reformers began to make new nets. That was their mistake.

Christ had made the original net, and had said that it would never fail. And it has not failed. The Catholic Church is as vital as ever. It is she today who defends the Bible; who stands for the fundamental Christian doctrines; who refuses all compromise where the moral law is in question. But the new nets or Churches made by the Reformers are rapidly going to pieces. The strands are broken, and the fish are swimming off in any direction they please, losing their faith in Christianity altogether.

Why are not Christians united?

God will not take away the gift of freewill and personal responsibility from any man. As for good people who still adhere to mistaken forms of Christianity, we can account for that only by the limitations of the human mind which render it so liable to error, and so little able to comprehend things in all their aspects. They concentrate on some good element retained in their mistaken form of religion, and lose sight of the aspects wherein it fails.

Christ Himself foresaw and predicted such divisions. "There will arise false Christs," He said, "to deceive if possible even the elect." Matt. 24; 24 And St. Paul warned Timothy, "There shall be a time when they will not endure sound doctrine; but, according to their own desires, they will heap to themselves teachers, having itching ears; and will indeed turn away their hearing from the truth, but will be turned unto fables." 2 Tim. 4; 3-4

I cannot adopt any definite profession of faith because the heads of all the different Churches disagree. How can I resolve this problem?

If they disagree, that shows at most that you cannot take their word on behalf of their own churches. But it does not follow that there is not a right church amongst them all. Your duty is to inquire, and find the church Christ actually established.

How is it possible to believe all the religions that claim to be true?

It is not possible. If any one of them is right, then the others are not. It can be proved historically that Christ lived, that He was God, and that He founded an imperishable Church, which was to be one, holy, catholic, and apostolic. Find that Church and you will have the true religion of Christ.

How can we solve the problem as to which is the true religion of Christ?

There are many ways of approaching the problem. But the simplest way is the historical way. Christ founded a Church and said the gates of hell or forces of evil would never prevail against it. Christ promised that His Church would not err. He said that He would be with it all days till the end of the world. So His Church must be still in this world and it must have been in the world all days since His time. That rules out all other Churches except the Catholic Church; for all other Churches came into existence long after Christ.

If I looked at this problem objectively, how could I recognize the true Church of Christ, and what signs should I look for?

The Church founded by Christ, its doctrine preached by the Apostles, still lives in the word today, according to the solemn promise of Christ Himself. Matt. 28; 20 It is the true Church, and the one Christ commanded all men to hear: "but if he refuse to hear even the Church, let him be to thee as the heathen and publican." Matt.

18; 17 But, as there are many imitations, many human societies claiming to be the Church Christ founded, it is very important to be able to distinguish Christ's Church from the others. The Council of Nice in the year 325 embodied in the Nicene Creed the words: "I believe in One, Holy, Catholic and Apostolic Church." The Church that has these four marks must be the true Church.

What do you mean by four marks of the Church?

The Church of Jesus Christ must be ONE, for Christ is Truth and Truth is One. He cannot contradict Himself. "Thou art Peter," He said, "and upon this rock I will build My Church, and the gates of hell shall not prevail (triumph) against it." Matt. 16; 18 He did not say "churches" but "Church," thus showing plainly that He meant to found one, and only one Church.

Reason itself tells us that God, who is absolute Truth, could not be the author of different churches, teaching contradictory doctrine in His name, else He would be responsible for the errors of unbelief. "One Lord, one faith, one baptism, one God and Father of all," says St. Paul in his letter to the Ephesians (IV; 5, 6) There is but one church in the world today that has unity and that is the Catholic Church.

According to statistics, there are over 700,000,000 Catholics, scattered through every part of the known world. They all worship the same God in the same way, through the holy sacrifice of the Mass, believe the same truths revealed by Jesus Christ, receive the same seven sacraments, and are united under one and the same spiritual head, forming the kingdom of Jesus Christ on earth. What a glorious kingdom! How vast its extent! And yet how closely united and beautifully coordinated! All its members receive the same spiritual life from their Head Jesus Christ, and all are governed and guided by one visible Chief Shepherd, the infallible Pope.

A recent report of the Census Bureau of Religious Bodies, indicates that less than half the people of the

The Catholic Church

United States belong to any Church and of these, more than 40% are Catholics. The rest are divided into 256 denominations and sects. Thus there are 21 kinds of Methodists, 21 kinds of Baptists, 12 kinds of Lutherans, 10 kinds of Presbyterians, 5 kinds of Adventists, 5 kinds of Reformed, 3 kinds of Unitarians, etc., etc.

Christ would not let His Church go to pieces in this way! Unity was to be one of its essential characteristics. How earnestly He prayed for unity on the eve of His bitter Passion and Death! "That all may be one, even as Thou, Father, in Me, and I in Thee; that they also may be one in us; that the world may believe that Thou hast sent Me." John 17; 21 "Holy Father, keep in Thy Name those whom Thou hast given Me; that they may be one even as We are." John 17; 11

How earnestly St. Paul insists on the eternal truth! The sins of disunion, heresy, and schism he classes with drunkenness, fornication and murder, and says those who are guilty of dissensions and sects shall not obtain the kingdom of God. Gal. V; 20, 21 To the Corinthians he writes, "I beseech you, brethren . . . that you all say the same thing, and that there be no dissensions among you," I Cor. 1; 10 and elsewhere in the same epistle, "Because the bread is one, we though many, are one body, all of us who partake of the one bread." Cor. 10; 17 And again, "You are the body of Christ, member for member." Cor. 12; 27 To the Galatians he writes, "If any one preach a gospel to you other than that which you have received, let him be anathema." Gal. 1; 9

Quotations from this great Apostle could be multiplied indefinitely, showing how emphatically he insists on that absolute unity which must always and everywhere characterize the true Church of Christ, and of which the Catholic Church alone has always been a singular and striking example, a unity which becomes all the more manifest as centuries pass.

Could you please explain how the Catholic Church is holy?

Holiness is one of the most glorious marks of the Catholic Church. A church that is not holy has no reason for existing, because the object of religion is to assist men to live good, pure, and holy lives in this world, and so prepare them for everlasting happiness in heaven. St. Peter called the Christians of his time "a chosen race . . . a holy nation, a purchased people." I Peter 2; 9

Could you explain what you mean more in detail?

The Catholic Church is holy:
1. Because her founder Jesus Christ is pre-eminently holy, and she teaches His doctrine whole and entire.
2. Because she faithfully preserves and dispenses all the means of holiness instituted by Christ.
3. Because at all times she has within her fold many great saints and martyrs whose sanctity God confirms by miracles, and numerous souls who practice the Gospel counsels.

The Catholic Church must be holy because Jesus Christ, the foundation of all holiness is her very life. He it is who makes His children holy by communicating to them His own Divine life, His grace and His merits, infusing into their souls His own holiness through the Mass and the seven sacraments. These are so many wonderful channels through which abundant grace and sanctification are conveyed to the souls of His living members, making them holy and pleasing to God.

What is the meaning of the word Catholic, and why was that name selected?

It is hardly necessary to show that the Church is Catholic or universal. Her very name proclaims it.

Christ came. He was a "catholic," that is, a "universal" teacher of Divine revelation to mankind. His Gospel was not only for the Jews, for Palestine, and for the first cen-

The Catholic Church

tuties but for all men of all times and all places. Christ's official commission to His Apostles was: "Go, therefore, and make disciples of all nations ... teaching them to observe all things that I have commanded you; and behold, I am with you all days, even to the consummation of the world." Matt. 23; 19, 20 Here we have from the lips of Christ Himself the assurance that His Church will be universal in time, in place and in doctrine.

The Catholic Church is the only Church in the world that has, and always has had this threefold universality. She is the only Church in the world today that can be historically traced back through every age, to the time of Christ and the Apostles. From their time down to our own, she has existed, taught and labored in every age.

Likewise, she is universal in place. Christ assigned to the Apostles the whole world as the theater of their labors. Geographically, the whole world has ever since continued to be the field in which the Catholic Church has labored. Go into every country of America, Europe, Asia, Africa and Australia, and everywhere you will find the Catholic Church. Everywhere she is equally at home, regardless of the form of government, the language, color or nationality of the people to whom she ministers. Like Christ, she has the same message for the poor and the rich, the learned and the unlettered, the saint and the sinner, for all men, in all places, and in all times.

Protestant Churches are scattered around the world. Couldn't they be called Catholic or Universal too?

No. The Protestant Churches are not universal in these three ways, nor in any one of them. Historically we know none of them were even in existence during the first fifteen hundred years of the Christian era; therefore they could not have been spread over any part of the earth at all, at least not during that long period.

But are not all Protestant Churches universal in matters of doctrine?

Far from it! They are anything but that, for they are built upon the principal of private interpretation of the Bible. Each has a different interpretation of the Scriptures; and what is more painful still, these same divergences are found among different members of the same sect. Now, private judgment and private interpretation are simply incompatible with sound doctrine. When fallible private opinion is substituted for doctrine and dogma, is it any wonder that within the same sect can be found all manner of contradictory opinions and teachings even about the most fundamental truths of Christianity?

What do you mean by "Apostolic", and what does it have to do with the Apostles?

When we say the Church is apostolic we mean that it has come down by an unbroken succession of pastors from the Apostles, and received its mission, holy orders and doctrine from them. Christ Himself chose the Apostles, and made them, with St. Peter as their chief, the foundation of His Church. He solemnly commissioned them to preach His doctrine and establish His Church. Hence the Church they preached and planted must be the only true and apostolic Church; and any Church that cannot trace its origin to them cannot be the true Church.

Christ made St. Peter chief of the Apostles, and visible head of His Church, and from that day to this there has been a long and unbroken line of Popes who have ruled the Catholic Church as the lawful successors of St. Peter. The Catholic Church's doctrine, likewise, cannot be traced to any one man or group of men, nor to any particular country or date other than apostolic times and apostolic authority. She received and guarded the writings of the Apostles and thus formed the canon of the New Testament. She preserves as priceless treasures the bodies and relics of the Apostles, which rest under her altars and in her great basilicas.

Christ established a religion that all Churches can lay claim to, which was the Church of the New Testament, isn't this true?

Absolutely not!

No Protestant denomination can have any possible claim to going back to the time of Christ. They cannot go back farther than their founders. The truth of the matter is that all of them were founded, not by Christ and His Apostles, but by inconstant and fallible men. Most of them came, directly or indirectly, from Luther's revolt in 1517; none of them are more than four hundred years old; many of them originated still more recently, even within the last century; and they continue to split up.

It is not a matter of indifference to what denomination a person belongs. The Church which all must join, if they wish to please God and save their souls, is the holy Church which Christ founded; the united Church which teaches all His doctrines; the universal Church which is spread over the whole world; and the apostolic Church which goes back in unbroken succession to Christ and the Apostles. And that is the holy, Roman Catholic Church alone!

POINTS OF CATHOLIC TEACHING

Incorporated into the Church through Baptism, the faithful are consecrated by the baptismal character to the exercise of the cult of the Christian religion... Taking part in the Eucharistic Sacrifice which is the fount and apex of the whole Christian life, they offer the divine Victim to God and offer themselves along with It... Those who approach the Sacrament of Penance obtain pardon from the mercy of God for offenses committed against Him.

Second Vatican Council: *The Church*

THE EUCHARIST

What is the Holy Eucharist?

It is a Sacrament instituted by Christ, in which Christ Himself is truly, really and substantially present that He may be offered in the Holy Mass as the Sacrifice of the New Law, and also that He may be received by us in Holy Communion for the spiritual refreshment of our soul.

Are there any signs in the Host proving that He is bodily present?

No. It is a mystery of faith. All external appearances remain as before consecration, but the substance of bread and the substance of wine are changed into the substance of Our Lord's body and blood. The reason why we believe is not in the *Host* as such, but in *God*. He has revealed this truth, and we believe because He must know and could not tell an untruth.

Did not the Jews think that they were asked to eat the very body of Christ?

When Christ promised that He would give His very flesh to eat, the Jews protested because they imagined a natural and cannibalistic eating of Christ's body. Christ refuted this notion of the manner in which His flesh was to be received by saying that He would ascend into Heaven, not leaving His body in its human form upon earth.

But He did not say that they were not to eat His actual body. He would thus contradict Himself, for a little earlier He had said, "My flesh is meat indeed and My blood is drink indeed". He meant: "You will not be asked to eat My flesh in the horrible and natural way you think, for My body as you see it with your eyes will be gone from this earth; Yet I shall leave My flesh and blood in another and supernatural way which your natural and carnal minds cannot understand. I ask you therefore to have faith in Me and trust Me. It is the spirit of faith which will enable you to believe, not your natural judgment."

Then the Gospel goes on to say that many would not believe, and walked no more with Him; just as many today will not believe, and walk no more with Him; just as many today will not believe, and walk no more with the Catholic Church.

Have we only the word of the priest that Christ's body and blood are present in what you call the Consecrated Host?

No Catholic priest would himself believe it, were it not the doctrine of Christ. It would be the height of folly to believe in it without solid evidence that Christ had taught it. When Christ says "This is My body", we have to accuse Him of falsehood or else admit that it *is* His body, not according to the senses but according to the underlying substance which is imperceptible to the senses.

THE MASS

It is little use your telling us what ought to be unless you can prove it as a fact from Scripture.

I can do so. The Old Testament predicts that Christ

will offer a true sacrifice to God in bread and wine — that He will use these elements. And this prediction is every bit as clear as the prediction that He will also offer Himself upon the Cross. Thus *Gen. XIV tells us that Melchisedech was a priest, and later Christ is called a "Priest according to the order of Melchisedech"* (Ps. 110; 4), that is, offering a sacrifice which is the same as that of Calvary but which is offered in a different manner for the Crucifixion was not a Sacrifice under the forms of bread and wine.

You may say that Christ fulfilled the prediction at the Last Supper, but the rite was not to be continued. However, that admits that the rite was truly sacrificial — and the fact is that it has been continued in exactly the same sense. It was predicted that it would continue. After foretelling the rejection of the Jewish priesthood, the prophet Malachy predicts a new sacrifice to be offered in every place.

"From the rising of the sun even to the going down my name is great among Gentiles: and in every place there is sacrifice and there is offered to my name a clean oblation." (Mal. 1, 10-11) The sacrifice of Calvary took place in one place only. We must look for a sacrifice re-presenting Calvary, one offered in every place under the forms of bread and wine. The Mass is that Sacrifice.

For a true Sacrifice we need a Priest, an altar, a victim and a convenant with God. Christ was truly the Great High Priest, and He gave the power of Priests to His Apostles, commissioning them to do repeatedly as He Himself had done in their presence. "Do this," He said, "in commemoration of me".

Power was to persevere in the Church, as Malachy had predicted. As victim, Christ offered Himself at the Last Supper. *Taking bread and wine He said, "This is My body ... This is My blood ... As often as you shall eat this bread and drink this chalice, you shall show the death of the Lord until He come."* (1 Cor. XI; 24-26) The separate forms of consecration represented the separation of His body and blood when He ratified the Sacrifice by His death on the Cross the next day. The victim then is Christ under the appearances of bread and wine representatively separated. This does not interfere with the value of Calvary, for Christ's real death occured there.

Continuously throughout the ages the Sacrifice of the Mass has been offered daily in the Catholic Church and is today offered in every place from the rising of the sun even to its going down, as Malachy predicted. Every day, that is every 24 hours, there are thousands of priests saying Holy Mass at the same time. Can anything be plainer to understand?

CONFESSING SINS

Why should I confess my sins to a fellow man, when I can go directly to God? I don't need a priest to forgive me.

Christ and His Church have specified the terms for forgiveness. Since God is doing the forgiving, He alone has the right to place the requirements for exercising this power. This He did when He said to the apostles, *Whose sins you shall forgive, they are forgiven them; and whose sins you shall retain, they are retained.* (John 20; 23) This choice of the apostles and their successors in the priesthood indicates that the sins must be heard to judge whether to forgive or not forgive them.

It surprises many persons to learn that a priest must sometimes refuse to use the power given to him because the sinner does not prove he has true sorrow for having offended God. The penitent must have the sincere intention to avoid the occasion of sin. Anyone who sincerely repents will receive forgiveness.

Catholics are expected to follow the way Christ pointed out. It is very understandable how perfectly reasonable it is for anyone to shy away from the completely erroneous idea held by many persons. Some think, for instance, that the penitent is known to the confessor, causing much embarrassment. (They forget the confidences shared with doctors and attorneys.) The priest is bound by the seal of confession to keep everything mentioned in the confessional a secret.

Thousands of Protestants have visited Catholics Churches and have seen the confessionals. They have noticed the separate compartments for priest and penitent. They have learned that the priest cannot see the one confessing, that names are never revealed and that sordid details of sin are omitted. These facts knock out the old idea of the "hold" which priests are supposed to acquire, especially when it is remembered that Catholics may confess their sins to any of the thousands of priests available.

Then there are some who actually believe that we Catholics pay a priest to have our sins forgiven. I have placed five thousand dollars on deposit at the First Federal Loan Association in Russels Point, Ohio, in my name, if it can be proven that any priest in good standing with the Church accepted money from any person for forgiveness of their sins.

The Church law sometimes allows face-to-face confession, and recent regulations make explicit provision for them, but penitents are always free to choose the way they wish to confess.

In confession we kneel, as it were, at the foot of the cross while the sacred blood of Christ washes our soul so that it may be "whiter than snow." In this encounter with the crucified Savior He helps us to achieve repentance. The flow of His love in the divinely-instituted sacrament strengthens our determination to live for Christ.

If the forgiveness of sins required only that we "accept Christ" or declare personal reformation, then our Lord would never have instituted forgiveness of sins by His priests. There are many new converts to Catholicism who were going through life with the burden of a past sin pressing them down. They have rejoiced because in the Catholic Church they found the means of escaping the heavy yoke and starting anew.

PRIESTS FORGIVE SINS

How can a priest forgive sins?

Confession was instituted by Christ on the first Easter evening when He said to St. Peter and the Apostles: *He said therefore to them again: "Peace be to you. As the Father hath sent me, I also send you".* (John 20; 21) And then as if to clear up all doubt as to His power He immediately adds, *Whose sins you shall forgive, they are forgiven them; and whose sins you shall retain, they are retained.* (John 20; 23).

The promise of Christ to Peter was: *And I will give to thee the keys of the kingdom of heaven. And whatsoever thou shalt bind upon earth, it shall be bound in heaven: and whatsoever thou shalt loose on earth, it shall be loosed also in heaven.* (Matt. 16; 19)

Was this pardoning power to cease with the Apostles? By no means. The nature of the Catholic Church, which is the representative of Christ to continue His work until the end of the world shows that the pardoning power was not a personal gift to the Apostles alone, but a permanent institution, to last until the end of time. *Teaching them to observe all things whatsoever I have commanded you: and behold I am with you all days, even to the consummation of the world.* (Matt. 28; 20)

ATTENDING MASS

Why are Catholics compelled to attend Mass on Sundays and other Holy Days?

Because all peoples, regardless of their religion, owe God the definite, regular, and public acknowledgment of their indebtedness to Him by public worship in the practice of their religion, and in our case, the Holy Sacrifice of the Mass is the highest act of worship we can give Him.

You must remember that religion is a form of justice, by which we render to God what we owe Him. Catholics are compelled to fulfill the duties of their religion just as honest people feel compelled to pay their just debts to their fellow men. The fact that they have real obligations does not affect the fact that their fulfillment of them is voluntary.

God exacts religious acknowledgment. He tells us to keep holy the Sabbath Day. Now Catholics don't want to be unjust to God, and their Church tells them that they will be unjust to God unless they attend Mass on the days appointed. So we give God adoration, thanksgiving, expiation of our sins, and the acknowledgment of our dependence on Him by offering prayers of petition.

Matters of attending public worship, regardless of one's religion should not be taken lightly, such as omitting duties of religion altogether; or going to Church only when one happens to feel like it, or turning to God only when things go wrong. We Catholics say, "Its not a matter of what is pleasant, not merely of what is useful; it's a matter of what is right".

CATHOLIC CEREMONIES

Why do Catholics have so many silly and meaningless ceremonies? Can't Christians worship God without so much ceremony?

If our ceremonies appear silly and meaningless to you, it is because you do not understand their beautiful symbolism. Not a word is said, nor gesture made, not an action performed in the Catholic Church, but is intended to raise the soul to God, and to foster and increase our love for Him.

Ceremony is natural to man. The soul is always under the influence of the senses, which are apt to draw away from the contemplation of the things of God. Does it not seem natural that a Church that appeals to the whole man, as God's Church does, should make the senses aid in the awakening of spiritual thoughts, and the driving away of worldly distractions?

Man expresses outwardly what he feels interiorly. His handshake expresses friendship, his kiss expresses love, his blow is evidence of his anger. Should we not then give outward expression to our friendship and love of God, and our hatred of all things opposed to Him?

The Old Law and the Gospels are full of ceremonies described in detail. *Christ knelt in prayer.* (Luke 22; 41) *He fell flat on the ground.* (Mark 14; 35) *He raised His eyes to heaven in giving thanks.* (Mark 6; 41) *He cured the deaf and dumb man by putting His finger into his ears and spitting He touched his tongue.* (Mark 7;33;34) *He cured the blind man, spitting on the ground and making a clay of the spittle.* (John 9; 6) *He breathed upon the Apostles.* (John 20; 22) *And the Apostles anointed the sick with oil.* (Mark 6; 13) *The Apostles baptized with water.* (Acts 2; 41) *Imposing hands in ordination.* (Tim. 4; 14) *They used relics to work miracles.* (Acts. 19; 12) *And they performed symbolic actions.* (Acts 21; 11)

By what right does the Catholic Church make laws which bind Catholics under pain of sin?

The Catholic Church has the right to make laws from Jesus Christ, who founded the Church and who said to the first Bishop of His Church: *Amen I say to you, whatsoever you shall bind upon earth, shall be bound also in heaven; and whatsoever you shall loose upon earth, shall be loosed also in heaven.* (Matt. 18; 18) This legislative authority of the Church is known as "the power of the keys" and it includes everything necessary for the government of the Church and for the guidance of the faithful. The primary purpose of Church laws is the eternal salvation of men.

Why do Catholics cross themselves when they go into Church or before they eat a meal? Oh yes, it seems they do it every time they say prayers.

Catholics begin their prayers and sanctify their actions by the sign of the cross, because it is the symbol of our redemption by Jesus Christ.

Why do Catholics sprinkle themselves with holy water in their homes and before entering the Church?

Catholics use holy water to call to mind the purity of heart with which they should come into the presence of Christ, really present upon the altar. In blessing it, the priest adds some salt to symbolize incorruption and immortality. The use of holy water is in no way a superstitious practice, its efficacy depends entirely upon the devotion of those who use it, and upon God's acceptance of the prayers of His Church.

Why do you burn candles before shrines of the saints, and around the bodies of the dead?

In Christian tradition the clean wax of the candle is

symbolic of the pure flesh of Christ, the wick an image of the soul of Christ, and the flame a figure of the divine personality of the Word made Flesh. *That was the true light, which enlighteneth every man that cometh into this world.* (John 1; 9) *Again therefore, Jesus spoke to them, saying: I am the light of the world: he that followeth me, walketh not in darkness, but shall have the light of life.* (John 8; 12) *So let your light shine before men, that they may see your good works, and glorify your Father who is in heaven.* (Matt. 5; 16) The candles that burn before the shrines are symbolic of prayer and sacrifice. Those that burn around the dead symbolize the faith of the Catholic, manifested before men by his good works.

IMAGES AND STATUES

The Bible expressly says, "Thou shall not make to thyself any graven image or anything in the heaven above, or in the earth beneath. Thou shalt not bow down to them nor worship them". Why then are Catholic Churches decorated with images and statues, when in the Bible it forbids it?

The text you seem to mean is: *Thou shalt not make to thyself a graven thing, nor the likeness of any things, that are in heaven above, or that are in the earth beneath, or that abide in the waters under the earth.* (Deut. 5;8) But if you had read the following verse, it would have explained itself. *Thou shalt not adore them, and thou shalt not serve them.* (Deut. 5;9) God does not forbid the making of images, in fact, He directs just the opposite. *Thou shalt make also two cherubims of beaten gold, on the two sides of the oracle. Let one cherub be on the one side, and the other on the other side. Let them cover both sides of the propitiatory, spreading their wings, and covering the oracle and let them look one towards the other, their faces being turned towards the propitiatory wherewith the ark is to be covered.* (Exod. 25; 18; 19; 20).

We Catholics are not so foolish as to adore images and statues. As you can see from the above texts, God forbids men to make images and then adore them. He orders the making of two angels out of beaten gold to stand on the two sides of the oracle. He also directs that the angels should be standing so their wings cover the oracle. Would you accuse God of not knowing the sense of His own law?

Catholics do honor representations of those who are in heaven, just as we all honor our dead soldiers by tributes of respect. If I lift my hat to the flag of my country as I pass the memorial to our dead soldiers, am I honoring the cloth or the stone, or what it stands for? If it is lawful in that case, it is certainly lawful to honor the memorials of the dead heroes of Christianity, the Saints.

INDULGENCES

I have heard Catholics speak of "indulgences." What are they?

Do not mix up the ecclesiastical term with the modern idea of self indulgence. An indulgence is not a permission to indulge in sin, but is a remission of punishment due to sin. In the early Christian Church certain sins were punished by long public penance, sometimes for days at other times for years. But the Church was often indulgent, and loosed or freed Christians from all or part of their public penance, if they showed other good dispositions, or performed certain works of charity. The Church had that power in the name of God as the state has the power in its own name to commute a sentence or even release a criminal altogether under certain circumstances.

Christ said to His Church, "Whatsoever you shall loose upon earth shall be loosed in heaven." (Matt. 18; 18) That power of commuting or even of remitting penance and expiation exists in the Church today, being exercised by the granting of indulgences.

What is a plenary indulgence?

A plenary indulgence remits all the punishment due to our sins. If one gained a plenary indulgence perfectly at the hour of death, he would be exempt from any purification in purgatory. Such an indulgence would not increase one's merit, but would merely free from the penalties due to past sins. The conditions for the gaining of a plenary indulgence are as a rule earnest prayer for the Pope's intentions, and often, Confession and Communion.

Can an indulgence be applied to the souls in purgatory?

Yes, but by God alone. We can but ask Him to accept indulgences on their behalf. But we can certainly offer them with a definite conviction of their acceptance by God for those we love, even as we share our goods in this life with needy friends. This is implied by the doctrine of the Communion of Saints.

CATHOLICS AND MASONS

Why are Catholics forbidden to become Masons?

No matter how tolerant individual Masons may be toward the Catholic Church, and with due charity towards individual Masons, the Church still does not encourage Catholics to join the Masonic Lodge for many and good reasons. The Catholic Church's and the Masonic Lodges's moral principles are not the same.

A letter from the Prefect of the Sacred Congregation for the Doctrine of the Faith (July 18, 1974) effects a change in the absolute prohibition of Catholics joining Masonic societies. The chief points of the letter are:

1. The Church still does not encourage Catholic membership in Masons.
2. Clergy, religious, and members of secular institutes are still forbidden, in every case, from joining any Masonic association.
3. Catholic laymen are not forbidden to hold membership in Masonic orders where the individual lodge is not anti-Catholic. (This can be judged from whether or not the actual attitude and practice of a lodge shows active hostility to the Church.)
4. The penalty of excommunication (Canon Law 2335) in case of membership in secret societies actively hostile against the Church is applicable only in instances of such hostility.

From what I have learned in the United States, the Lodge does not take a stand against the Church. In fact, I have some very good friends that are Masons. There is a wonderful spirit of fellowship between the Masons and the Knights of Columbus in our own area. We even have joint banquets together each year. We take turns being hosts to each other. It is our joint hope that someday in the future the veil between both orders will be lifted, so an even closer unity will be ours.

BIBLE

Did not Christ promise that He would send the Holy Spirit to teach us all the truth of Scriptures?

He did not promise that the Holy Spirit would teach each individual separately. If every individual were under the guidance of the Holy Spirit, all who read Scripture sincerely should come to the same conclusion. But they do not. The frightful chaos as to the meaning of Scripture is proof positive that the Holy Spirit has not chosen this way of leading men to the truth. It is blasphemy to say that the Holy Spirit does not know His own mind, and that He deliberately leads men into contradictory notions. Christ promised to preserve His Church by the guidance of the Holy Spirit, and only in the Church which shows signs of having been preserved in the ways of holiness and in the knowledge of revealed truth are men sure of finding the correct teaching.

In our day, there is no whim, fad or fancy that someone does not claim to prove from the Bible. Almost any man or woman can set himself up as a competent interpreter of the word of God.

Just what do you mean by Bible vandalism? Are you saying that Scriptures are deliberately interpreted by some people to suit their own purpose?

Yes, Some like the early heretics, will prove from the Bible that Christ is only God and not man. Others, will prove from the Bible that Christ is only man and not God.

Some denominations will prove from the Bible that in the New Law, Christ shared His priesthood with NO ONE. Others will prove from the Bible that in the New Law even women can be priests.

One sect will prove from the Bible that baptism is unnecessary for children but is necessary for adults. Others will prove from the Bible that baptism is necessary for no one; that it is only a ceremony, an initiation such as when you join a lodge.

Some will prove from the Bible that to be really baptized, one must be totally immersed in water. Others prove from the Bible that the whole thing is unnecessary and ought to be abandoned.

Points of Catholic Teaching

Some prove from the Bible that there is going to be a millennium, a thousand years when every one will get a second trial. Some will prove from the Bible that a large part of mankind do not even get a first trial, but are predestined to damnation irrespective of their merits.

Some prove from the Bible that eternal punishment is going to be meted out to nearly every one. Only the little handful of their particular sect is going to escape. Others prove from the Bible that everyone is going to be saved. Even murderers, adulterers, and those who rob widows and orphans, and never repent. In spite of all this, Christ will hold out His arms and say: "Come, Blessed of My Father, and possess the Kingdom prepared for you from the foundation of the world".

Some will prove from the Bible that man is all soul, the body is practically a delusion, and does not really exist. Some Bible Students will prove from the Bible that the soul is all delusion, you really have none.

The Bible itself warns us: "There shall come a time when men will no longer endure sound doctrine, but as with itching ears, will run after their own desires."

The dangers of any type of Scripture self-interpretation, even in excellent faith, become evident if we consider that the most obvious meaning of a Gospel verse may not in fact be the meaning the writer had in mind.

Before the Gospels, as we have them now, were written down, there were at first only partial accounts of the good news of salvation. Then various authors composed various writings and, finally, our present Gospels emerged and were accepted by the Church as inspired.

In the endeavor of Scripture scholars to grasp exactly what the Gospels mean, one of the most useful scholarly tools is what is called "form criticism," by which is meant the study of the Gospels from the point of view of a number of "situations" which illuminate the bare words of the text. Form criticism is of considerable importance for a correct understanding of the word of God — but it is likely seriously to undermine any attempt at self-interpretation.

Form criticism takes into account the socio-historical circumstances which gave rise to each Gospel in general and to this or that passage in particular. Was there a special challenge to some doctrine at that time? Were there especially-energetic persecutions or dangers of defection?

It is vital to recall that, before a line of any Gospel was written, there existed vigorous stream of oral tradition. Years of preaching, discussing, instructing and pastoral service had passed. The Gospels are the officially written word of God but the unwritten word pre-dated them, influenced their formation and now affects their interpretation.

Besides the "life situation" there is the "situation in the Gospel, "by which is meant how the Evangelist wrote his text, what was his purpose, how he arranged his material and on what oral and written sources did he draw. (For example: Matthew shows Our Lord giving a long and famous "Sermon on the Mount" — possibly because he liked to put similar points together as an aid to memory. Luke uses much of the same material but has Jesus speak it at different times).

There is also the fact that the Evangelists adapted the words of Our Lord to the needs of their own times. The community of Christians to whom they addressed their efforts was much larger and more diversified than the little group present at the first Pentecost. Matthew, for example, is the only one to add the words" . . . except for immorality . . ." to our Lord's remarks about divorce and he also

Points of Catholic Teaching

puts into Jesus' mouth strong sayings against the Jews which may represent more the problems of the Church forty years after Jesus' death than His own attitude during life.

Much more could be written but the point is quite clear: basing a whole life or an important decision on a phrase or two from Scripture, without knowing a good deal more than meets the eye or without accepting the guidance of a competent authority, is an extremely risky business.

POINTS OF CATHOLIC MORALITY

In the formation of their consciences the Christian faithful ought carefully to attend to the sacred and certain doctrine of the Church. The Church is, by the will of Christ, the Teacher of the truth. It is her duty to give utterance to, and authoritatively to teach, that Truth which is Christ Himself, and also to declare and confirm by her authority those principles of the moral order which have their origin in human nature itself.

> Second Vatican Council: *Declaration on Religious Freedom*

BIRTH CONTROL

Why is the Catholic Church so opposed to birth control and will the Pope have to give in to birth control for all Catholics?

The Catholic Church and the Pope are not opposed to the controlling of the number of children by lawful means. But they are opposed to birth control as commonly understood to mean the prevention of conception by artificial means. Newspapers, magazines and TV Talk Shows continue to have a holiday in criticizing the Catholic Church and especially the Pope for blocking the progress in liberalism in birth control for Catholics.

There are a great number of people, also many Catholics, who actually believe that the next Pope will relax, or even possibly do away with the present birth control laws. This will never happen and to anyone who thinks that the next Pope might be more liberal on this issue, I say "Forget it". It will never change, or even be modified as long as conception is prevented by artificial means of any kind.

To learn and understand the attitude of the Church concerning the issue at hand, we must refer to the Old Testament. We must not forget that God is the author of all moral laws and artificial birth control is contrary to that law.

An act that was a crime and a destestable thing in the eyes of God thousand of years ago is still a crime and a detestable thing today. This is not an ecclesiastical law of the Church that can be modified or changed, but a divine law made by God Himself. No power on earth can ever dispense man from it. The Catholic Church and the Pope are not here to allow its people to break God's laws but to see that they are kept, as far as possible.

The Church and the Pope cannot, or will not "water down" God's laws to suit the modernism trend that is saturating the morals of today. Do we expect the courts to "water down" our civil laws to humor or suit the law breaker, who would scream to "high heaven" that his "civil rights" have been violated, that the laws of the state are too strict, that the police and the judge should not enforce the laws?

Now, if this example about the lawbreaker can be understood, why is it so hard to understand the Pope's position and grave responsibility to interpret and enforce the laws of God?

ABORTION

Why do you Catholics fight our abortion laws so? Can't you just leave the Courts alone, and keep out of their business? Why do you try to force your doctrine on other people?

First of all, let it be understood that Catholics are not alone in the fight against abortion. There are millions of persons in the same fight from every race and creed. It is true, we Catholics have the anti-abortion label stamped more readily upon us, because our teaching authority is more vocal in condemning such a practice.

Points of Catholic Morality

Dr. Albert Schweitzer, one of the greatest humanitarians of our times once stated, "If you lose reverence for any part of life, you will lose reverence for all life." That is the very reason on which we base our deep concern. Don't you remember the words of our Constitution? "We hold these truths to be self-evident, that all men are created equal. They are endowed by their creator with certain inalienable rights. That among those are life, liberty and the pursuit of happiness".

The Supreme Court's decision to uphold abortion is an unspeakable tragedy for our nation. They have abused the powers and responsibilities of the legislation of all fifty states to protect human life. Up until now, abortion was a private concern between a mother and a doctor. Now, it has become a national crime and disaster, an indescribable calamity and a declaration of war on the unborn. Never since Hitler, has a nation put a price tag of social and economic usefulness on an individual human life as the price of the life of the unborn child and its inalienable right to existence. And it is to that right I call your attention, a right justified by God's commandment: "THOU SHALT NOT KILL".

We Americans are shocked at the inconsistency of the highest court in the land, which declared capital punishment unconstitutional and now licenses the slaughter of the unborn, helpless babies. The Supreme Court has perpetrated a dastardly system upon our nation.

To illustrate how inconsistant our Supreme Court laws are, a pregnant woman can have an auto accident, lose her baby by a natural abortion, sue for a vast amount of money and win her case, because the law claims that the baby in her womb was a living person. A child, itself, after he is born and being represented by an attorney, can sue for injuries prior to birth, and win! Yes, an unborn child can even get social security benefits, the right to inheritance, have a blood transfusion over his mother's objection, have a guardian appointed and other rights of citizenship. All of these are benefits by law, because the courts claim that the child in the womb is human and has all rights that any American Citizen has. Then the Supreme Court turns right around and then claims that a child in the womb under three months is a non-person and has no rights, so an abortion is legal if the mother wishes to have one.

It is estimated that the abortion mills in America kill over two million babies each year. That is more killing than all of the lives lost in all of the wars put together since we are a nation. Most abortions are done by one of these methods: Cutting the baby to pieces, limb by limb and even by decapitation of its little head. There is another type of abortion: abortion by hysterotomy. From a survey of 37,000 abortions, 1.3% were hysterotomy. Now get this: 100% of these abortions were born, breathing and weak, crying, thrown in a bucket or pan and left to die.

Aborted infants are often sent to a hospital pathology lab where they may be used for research purposes. Sometimes while still showing signs of life, infants have their organs removed, or are given massive doses of medication to keep them alive for later study. The Chief of pediatrics of a hospital in the State of New York injects chemicals into umbilical cords of fetuses. While the heart is still beating, he removes their heads, lungs, liver and kidneys for study. It is a matter of record that in one of the major hospitals, a baby was dissected without an anesthesia before he died.

We Americans have no choice but to urge that the Court's judgment be opposed and rejected, and every legal possibility must be explored to challenge this murderous slaughter of human life. To keep silent is nothing less than permissiveness. We must speak out, protest violently against the Supreme Court, which has made a mockery of moral law. Unless this hideous and abominable crime is condemned and rectified, we are headed straight on a collision course with the wrath of God. This heinous transgression is crying to heaven for vengence.

What has the Bible to say about killing the innocent? *Cursed be he that taketh pay, to slay an innocent person.* (Deut. 27; 24; 25).

SOME LITTLE-KNOWN FACTS

Here are some facts that can't be ignored. There is no more fascinating study in life than investigation of life itself: the perpetuation of living organisms which involves the processes of growth and development of a human being from conception to birth. Being a layman, I can rely only on what I read in books of medical science published by the Life Science Library, on the growth of cells of human beings.

The authors of these Medical Science Books are: James Tanner, M.D. (he calls himself a "human biologist" and is an authority on physical growth and development from the John Hopkins Medical School), Dr. Gordon Taylor, a graduate of Trinity Medical College, an eminent writer noted for his books on the Science of Life; Dr. René Dubos, professor of Rockefeller University, distinguished microbiologist; Eugene Higgins, professor of Physics at Yale; Dr. Snow, author of the "Effects of Science on Today's Society".

All of these Medical Scientists unanimously agree that a new life begins at conception. They refer to the embryo as human and having life. Conception takes place when the male sperm meets the female ovum. This is known as the embryo. The embryonic period extends from 55 to 57 days, when the body structure is completed. The embryo is known as the fetus and their claim is that at the moment of conception, a new human life is created. The September 1970 issue of the California Medical Journal stated that it's a "scientific fact" that human life begins at conception.

In its special issue "The Drama of Life Before Birth", Life magazine states, "The birth of a human being really occurs at the moment the mother's egg cell is fertilized by one of the father's sperm cells". That is at the moment of conception.

Now, who do you think is the most qualified to determine when life really begins, the Supreme Court or these eminent medical men named in the above? It would seem to me that the Supreme Court who have the very weighty and intricate problems and decisions of the nation in their hands, would have done as much research in the issue of abortion as they do in other matters of grave importance. They did not, and if they had given it the same amount of study and contemplation, more than seven billion little babies would be the ages of one, two and three years old now.

On January 24th, 1973, just two days after the Supreme Court's infamous decision. Chief Justice Blackmun hurried to apologize in public at the Cedar Rapids Chamber of Commerce for their too hasty and regrettable decision. There are not many people who know this but this was his statement: "The Court didn't have time to probe into the matter of abortion. We never have time to put our foot on the window sill and reflect". So we must assume that when Supreme Court Justice Blackmun hasn't time to rest his thinking foot on the window sill and ponder, he puts it in his mouth. Need I say more?

Do you know of someone who is planning to have an abortion? If you do, please give this some very serious thought. If this woman will allow her child to be born, her doctor and hospital expenses will be paid in full, providing she, the mother, will agree to give the baby out for adoption. There are many well respected young couples who will give it a good home and the mother can have her baby in any hospital she chooses. Complete and strict confidence will be respected. Neither the mother or the recipients of the child will have knowledge of the other's identity. Every aspect of the transaction will be legal and through a reputable adoption agency. Please notify the author, through the Publishers of this book. Immediate action will be taken to implement the above statements.

VASECTOMY

What about a vasectomy, isn't that another form of birth control?

Yes, very much so. A vasectomy, when done as a contraceptive procedure to render the male sterile is gravely immoral because it is a violation of the fifth and sixth commandments: It violates a man's duty to preserve both his bodily and functional integrity.

This type of operation is becoming quite common and acceptable among middle-class white males, although it is largely rejected by men of Black and Spanish origins. It is psychologically very dangerous for males who feel any way sexually challenged and each year some 20,000 try to have the operation reversed. The American Public Health Association advises doctors to warn patients that present surgical methods are almost universally irreversible.

HOMOSEXUALITY

How can you possibly condemn homosexuality as an act of perversion, when the doctors and psychiatrists claim that homsexuality is an affliction?

First of all, psychiatrists and doctors are not theologians, and psychologists should stay in their own field.

Theologians take the psychiatrists' and psychologists' findings and formulate pastoral counsel for people with homosexual problems to help them according to the degree of their freedom. Psychiatrists and psychologists are not qualified to tell anyone in their "infallible terminology" that homosexuality is a "way of life", equally as normal and virtous as the sacred heterosexual union of a man and a woman in marriage.

A distinction is drawn, and it seems with some reason, between homosexuals whose tendency comes from false education, from lack of normal sexual development, from habit, from bad example or from other similar causes, and is transitory or at least not incurable and homosexuals who are definitely such because of some kind of innate instinct or a pathological condition judged to be incurable. These homosexuals must certainly be treated with understanding and sustained in the hope of overcoming their personal difficulties and their inability to fit into society. Their culpability should be judged with prudence.

In Sacred Scripture homosexuality is condemned as a serious depravity and even presented as the sad consequence of rejecting God. This judgment of Scripture does not of course permit us to conclude that all those who suffer from this deviation of nature are all personally responsible for it, but it does attest to the fact that homosexual acts are disordered and can in no case be approved.

In the overall picture and condition of our country, sex perversion in all phases is more dangerous to the destiny of America, and for the whole world for that matter, than Atheism, Communism, military invasion or underground revolution. History tells us that the great empires of past ages have been destroyed by their perverse practices. These practices are moving in on our people like a great tidal wave and unless absolute measures of resistance are implemented by clergy of all denominations, who represent the influence and value of Christianity, we will sink into a pitch pit of moral chaos

Points of Catholic Morality

worse than the days of Sodom and Gomorrah. It is my hope that the Clergy, when they speak to their people, will open their Bible, get to the heart of the matter of homosexuality, and point out the texts that condemn it.

It seems that there is a concerted drive to have the Courts legalize homosexuality. Anyway, there are a lot of people who think it is an affliction. Some even say that these people are born that way. Let's see what the Bible has to say about it. *In Rom. 1; 26; "God therefore delivered them up to disgraceful passions. Their women exchanged natural intercourse for unnatural acts." In Rom. 1; 27; "And the men gave up natural intercourse with women and burned with lust for one another. Men did shameful things with men and thus received in their own persons the penalty for their perversions." In Lev. 18; 22; "Thou shalt not lie with mankind as with womankind; it is abomination".*

St. Paul specifically illustrates in his Epistle to the Romans that God distinctly deplores and condems moral depravity and corruption among men with men and women with women. At the time of Paul's writing, it was the pagan practice of homosexuality that provoked the Divine anger.

These people freely indulged in perverse desires. The wrath of God is revealed against the irreligious and perverse spirit of men and women who indulge in unnatural acts. St. Paul's letter to the Romans did not in any way indicate that God has double standards. God would not at one time refer to this act as perversion and abomination, then at another time excuse persons for the same act.

It seems that the whole issue involved in this controversy is the problem some have with fraternal charity. "How can I condemn anyone when only God can judge?" Nobody can condemn another *person*. The only thing that we can do and should do is condemn *evil actions*, objectively sinful actions. Anyone who believes in God and what is written in the Bible knows that homosexuality is a perversion of nature and is objectively a serious sin.

No psychiatrist can, or may, play this aberration down by saying that these people who do such acts have an irrestible tendency to these acts. If this were true, God would be unjust in inspiring St. Paul to write such a condemnation. When those who are not trained in Christian philosophy and theology usurp the right to moralize on human acts, they are wrong from the very start and are most unprofessional and dishonest.

Now as to the broad controversy of a person, responsible or not responsible for homosexuality, it is my firm belief that the awareness of one's own freedom before and during any act of homosexuality is such a universal, undeniable fact that it cannot be explained away as the result of mere ignorance of an unknown force, or affliction; it can only be explained by the reality of free will. The possibility of predicting with a high degree of accuracy, the future choices of individuals placed in certain circumstances, given the necessary opportunity to indulge in a perverse act, can only be explained by the fact that men usually choose that which is in accordance with their gradually cultivated habits.

EUTHANASIA

There seems to have been so much publicity about the Quinlan case, I am wondering what the Catholic Church would say about it?

For the benefit of those who are not familiar with the Quinlan case, here is a brief history of Karen Ann Quinlan who on April 14, 1975 was involved in an auto accident and was in a coma and sustained by a respirator for more than a year. Doctors said her brain damage was irreversible.

Points of Catholic Morality

In view of the prognosis, Karen's parents Mr. and Mrs. Joseph Quinlan, hoped that through court action they could terminate the life of the girl they adopted 21 years ago when she was just four weeks old. The attending physicians and the County Prosecutor opposed the family's request for "death with dignity" because they said that the turning off of the life-sustaining device would amount to murder.

Karen's case sparked a nationwide controversy over the legal question of "when does death occur?" Karen's parents said that religious freedom was at stake. As Catholics, they believed that no extraordinary life-sustaining mechanism needed to be used to keep her alive. That position was generally supported by Catholics, Protestants and Jewish Clergymen across the country, although some had reservations. Some thought that "a judgment of that type should be based on the quality of life and not just existence". There was a real question of whether the girl was really living or just existing. According to the doctor's intricate meters measuring brain waves, their determination was that Karen was biologically dead, with no chances for recovery.

Now in answer to your question "What does the Catholic Church say about it?" God has given each person an inviolable right to life and God explicitly forbids a person to take his own life or the life of another. Euthanasia is always a grave sin regardless of motives.

The Catholic Church is neither harsh nor heartless in this matter. She does not oppose the relief of suffering nor does She insist on the unnecessary prolongation of life. She does permit doctors, when they prudently judge a case hopeless, to abstain from the use of extraordinary measures to prolong life. She leaves the application of medical therapy to the professional judgment of the attending physician. It is one thing to inflict death directly; it is quite another thing to allow a natural death. The former is immoral; the latter is permissible when the patient is beyond cure.

The danger is that cases such as Karen Quinlan's may be the stepping stone to other experimentations with "life and death". It seems that there will be a concerted drive to put "euthanasia" into legislation as soon as possible.

We cannot treat people as we do animals. Euthanasia deprives the medical profession of the stimulus of research. There is little incentive for new discoveries in the treatment of disease if a quick death settles everything. Mercy-killing is an easy solution but it is all wrong.

Please don't be so optimistic as to believe that this can't happen in this country. Would it shock you to know that powerful forces are now at work trying to legalize these diabolic, barbaric practices? The killing of the elderly, the ill, the handicapped and the unwanted: this possibility grows stronger and your chances of dying a natural death grow smaller. Once you permit the killing of the unborn child, there will be no stopping. There will be no age limit.

If euthanasia is ever legalized, there will be a chain reaction that could eventually make you the victim. Your children, if they want to, can have you killed because you permitted the killing of their baby brothers and sisters. Your children, if they want to, can have you killed because they will not support if you are old and infirm. Your children, if they want to, can have you killed for your homes and estates. If a doctor will take money for killing the innocents in the womb, he will not hesitate to kill you with a needle when paid by your children.

The first steps have already being taken to put euthanasia into effect. Government Agents may yet have the power to deny you the right to choose your own doctor. You and your doctor may be denied the right to decide what medication is best for you. Confidentiality between you and your doctor may disappear. This is no figment of someone's imagination. Several states have pushed hard to put this into legislation.

Very few of the above facts have been printed in our magazines and daily newspapers. Someday you may be the older person — one of the "useless eaters" that are a burden on society. Would you want someone else to make the decision of whether you live or die?

DIVORCE

Why does the Catholic Church absolutely prohibit divorce? Is it not cruel and heartless to compel a woman to live with a drunken, adulterous husband, who refuses to support her? Would it not be more reasonable to allow exceptions in certain cases, as most states do?

First of all, let me clear up your first question. Brutal cruelty and ill-treatment are lawful grounds for separation, as also is adultery. But this separation does not break the bond of marriage. Death alone can do that, and neither is free to marry again whilst the other is still living. For grave reasons a Catholic can obtain ecclesiastical permission to have the separation rendered legal by civil decree of divorce in order to avoid legal difficulties, but this must be on the understanding that such a decree leaves neither party free to contract another marriage whilst the other party is still living.

In recent years ecclesiastical tribunals have been declaring that in a number of cases there never *was* a marriage. This is not a new procedure — it is simply being adopted more frequently.

The Bible teaches that lawful marriage cannot be dissolved by any human power. Christ's teachings are very clear that Christian marriage is indissoluble. *Therefore now they are not two, but one flesh. What therefore God hath joined together, let no man put asunder.* (Matt. 19; 6) Also, the Bible plainly teaches that remarriage during the lifetime of the former man or woman is adultery.

Every one that putteth away his wife, and marrieth another, committeth adultery: and he that marrieth her that is put away from her husband, committeth adultery. (Luke 16; 18)

St. Paul writes: "*And unto the married I command, yet not I, but the Lord, let not the wife depart from her husband; but if she depart let her remain unmarried, or be reconciled to her husband, and let not the husband put away his wife*". In short, the marriage bond cannot be dissolved because of adultery, or for any other reason on the part of either the husband or the wife; and neither party, not even the innocent one who gave no cause for the adultery, can contract another marriage while the other party is still living.

OTHER QUESTIONS

The Catholic Church, raising the torch of religious truth by means of this Ecumenical Council, desires to show herself to be the loving mother of all, benign, patient, full of mercy and goodness towards the brethren who are separated from her. ... The Church does not offer to the men of today riches that pass nor does she promise them a mere earthly happiness. But she distributes to them the goods of divine grace which, raising men to the dignity of sons of God, are the most efficacious safeguards and aids toward a more human life.

> Second Vatican Council: *Opening words of Pope John XXIII*

STATE AID FOR PAROCHIAL SCHOOLS

Why do you Catholics feel that you should receive State aid to operate your schools?

The national debate over education has focussed public opinion on the Catholic school system as never before in history. Reports about Catholic education range from the sound to the senseless. All fair-minded Americans should know the rightful place of Catholic schools in the United States.

Freedom of education, which is guaranteed by the First Amendment of the Constitution, means that parents have the right to choose to what accredited school they may send their children. The First Amendment states that no one shall be hindered in the free exercise of his religion. If taxes and government restrictions make it harder and harder for Catholic schools to operate, then Catholic parents are being denied this free exercise.

Because the Catholic school is doing a public service, Catholics feel that they have a right to a fair share of the benefits paid for by their school taxes. Any system of government aid which denies help to students in Catholic school is clearly unfair. Catholic parents are not asking non-Catholics to support their religion. They are asking for a fair return of the money they are already paying in taxes. This is not a *religious issue*. This is a question of *civil rights*. *Catholic* parents are subsidizing the education of *public school* children. The Catholic schools are making it possible for parents with children in public schools to get a free ride.

Some persons will say "The public schools are there for you Catholics to use. If you don't want to use them, that's your tough luck. Pay extra if you want your own schools." The facts are that there is not enough room in the public schools for all the Catholic children. Where would the public schools find room for 6,500,000 Catholic children now in Catholic schools? But more important, sending children to Catholic schools is not only a privilege, it is a right guaranteed by the Constitution of the United States. When a person has to pay extra to exercise a freedom then it is no longer free.

In the State of Ohio alone, Catholic schools save the tax payers an estimated $156,067,673 annually. Catholic parents have felt the pinch of taxes for many years and it is getting worse. They pay the same tax rate as their neighbors who send their children to public schools, but — they get none of their tax money back for the education of their own children.

How can fair-minded Americans continue to refuse to listen to the claims of Catholic parents? The survival of Catholic schools is important for the continuation of the free enterprise system in America.

By having their own schools, Catholic parents throughout the United States are making an annual contribution to the taxpayers equivalent to $3,200,000,000. The nation can hardly afford to see such a valuable contribution shrivel up because of discriminatory tax levies. It will be a sorry day in our country when taxation and financial discrimination push private schools out of business, so

THE POPE IS PETER

Granted that Peter was the chief of the Apostles and the head of the Church, appointed by Christ, how can you prove that His power was handed down through nineteen centuries? In other words, how can the Cardinals in your Church, only men, appoint a Pope, and that Pope, you claim to have the same power as Peter?

The Primacy of Peter was not a personal privilege, but an essential part of Christ's Church, the rock on which it was built. Christ established the office of Pope, as the head of His Church. The Cardinals elect and appoint the men to step into Peter's shoes. This procedure is clearly understood as the will of Christ Himself, who gave St. Peter the power of transmitting his privileges and authority as head of the Church by declaring that Church to be perpetual.

As a building is supported by its foundation, so the whole Church will ever rest upon the constitutional office and authority to be transmitted by Peter. Christ promised that His Church would remain till the end of time. He also promised that His Church would not err. If the Church is to remain all days till the end of the world, protected by Christ, it must remain just as He established it.

We have the same seven sacraments that Christ Himself gave us. We have the same sacrificial worship of God that must continue till the end of time. No one could alter the essential constitution He gave it, or it would no longer be the same Church. Upon Christ's own words, the Church is perpetual, and therefore, the office of Peter is to be transmitted to his successors down through almost two thousand years to our present Pope.

INFALLIBILITY

On what grounds do you hold that the Pope is infallible?

The Pope is the lawful successor of St. Peter, and therefore, inherits that privilege of St. Peter according to the will of Christ, who declared that the Church would not err and would last till the end of the world with the constitutional powers He gave it.

And I say to thee: That thou art Peter; and upon this rock I will build my church, and the gates of hell shall not prevail against it. And I will give to thee the keys of the kingdom of heaven. And whatsoever thou shalt bind upon earth, it shall be bound also in heaven: and whatsoever thou shalt loose on earth, it shall be loosed also in heaven. (Matt. 16; 18; 19)

The Pope is infallible ONLY when he defines faith and morals, which means to settle it definitely and finally. He is infallible when he speaks of faith and morals, which includes the whole content of divine revelation, or the deposit of faith, as St. Paul calls it.

Infallibility does not mean that the Pope is incapable of committing sin. He may commit sin like any other person, and he is bound like any other Catholic to use the sacrament of penance for forgiveness. Infallibility is not a personal, but a divine, official perogative given by Christ to Peter and his successors to keep them from error in teaching truths men must believe to be saved.

Just stop and think. Christ would have been a fool, with all of the suffering and torture He endured, and death on the cross, had He not put someone in charge to keep His teachings pure and free from error. We would have lost the Gospel message in one generation.

When He, the Spirit of truth, is come, He will teach you all truth. (John 16; 13) *The Paraclete, the Holy Ghost, whom the Father will send in my name, He will teach you all things, and bring all things to your mind, whatsoever I shall have said to you.* (John 14; 26) Here the Holy Ghost is promised to the Apostles and their successors, particularly, in order to teach them all truth, and to preserve them from error. *Behold, I am with you all days, even to the consummation of the world.* (Mat. 28; 20) Thus, Christ promised that the Holy Spirit would keep His Church from error and that He would be with us till the end of time.

PURGATORY

I am interested in your dogma concerning purgatory. Why make people afraid of such a horrible place, when you know that it does not exist? Is not this another one of your Catholic inventions?

No. If you can show me, when and where the Church invented this doctrine, I promise to spend the rest of my life exposing the Catholic Church as a merely human institution making outrageous claims upon men, and a fraud. The doctrine of purgatory, or a middle state of souls suffering for a time on account of their sins, is proved by those many texts of Scripture which affirm that God will render to every man according to his works: so that such as die in lesser sins shall not escape without punishment as can be found in the following text of the Bible.

Be at agreement with thy adversary betimes, whilst thou art in the way with him: lest perhaps the adversary deliver thee to the judge, and the judge deliver thee to the officer, and thou be cast into prison. Amen I say to thee, thou shalt not go out from thence till thou repay the last farthing. (Matt. 5; 25; 26)

I say to thee, thou shalt not go out thence, until thou pay the very last mite. (Luke 12; 58; 59)

Every man's work shall be manifest; for the day of the Lord shall declare it, because it shall be revealed in fire; and the fire shall try every Man's work, of what sort it is.

If any man's work abide, which he hath built thereupon, he shall receive a reward. If any man's work burn, he shall suffer loss; but he himself shall be saved, yet so as by fire. (Cor. 3; 13; 14; 15)

Let's suppose that I had stolen a thousand dollars from someone, that I died without paying back the money, or that I had not confessed my sins to God. Then let's suppose that you stole a penny from someone and died before paying back the penny, or that you had not had a chance to ask God for forgiveness. We all know that God is infinitely just, He will not allow anything defiled to enter heaven. Your sin is not as great as mine, and yet you cannot enter heaven until your soul has been cleansed. God certainly would not send you to hell for only stealing a penny, so there must be a middle place to pay off your debt to God. That central state of being is what we call purgatory. Webster's dictionary defines purgatory, as a place of purging.

I sincerely hope that I have made myself clear. Oh yes, there is another text that supports our doctrine on purgatory. *"It is therefore a holy and wholesome thought to pray for the dead that they may be loosed from their sins".* (Machabees 2; 12; 46)

WEALTH OF THE CHURCH

The extreme wealth of the Catholic Church is a scandal, with millions of starving people in the world. If Christ came to earth again, how would you explain to Him the reason for your magnificent, beautiful Cathedrals and Churches, when He was born poor and humble?

In the first place, not all Catholic churches are rich and beautiful. In mission countries they will often be bamboo and grass; in other isolated places, of wood, or

Other Questions

galvanized iron; or even of brick or stone, they will often lack the beautiful ornamentation of a Cathedral.

You speak of the great wealth of the Church. Would you say that a family is wealthy if it has scarcely enough to meet all its essential needs? The Catholic Church certainly has not enough for its necessary work. Meanwhile she spends millions on her many works for men's temporal welfare, and is very hard pressed to provide for her thousands of missionaries, who are laboring for the spiritual welfare of pagans, with the bare necessities of life.

Now in regard to the beautiful Cathedrals and Churches. If Catholics have erected beautiful buildings, those buildings have not been erected for any earthly gain. They have been erected to the honor and glory of Christ, Himself, so much do Catholics think of Him, and so ready are they for self-sacrifice in His cause.

Neither priests, bishops or the Pope own those buildings. These buildings are made possible by Catholic families of ordinary workers, families who have given their donations toward Churches, schools, rectories, convents and hospitals; families who have given their sons and daughters to fulfill the duties of religion and charity within them.

God ordered Solomon to build a magnificent temple. According to the description of it in the Bible, there was more gold in it than there is at Fort Knox. Don't you think that Christ would certainly agree with the beautifying of God's House?

THOSE "CHAINED" BIBLES

Why did the monks of the Middle Ages chain the Bible in their libraries and Churches?

The Bible and other books were chained in the libraries and Churches of the Middle Ages to preserve them from theft, and especially to make them accessible to students. In the Middle Ages there were no printing presses and all the Bibles had to be written by hand. Sometimes it took as long as ten years to complete just one. Don't you think that is a very good reason to chain a Bible in the back of a Church? Why does the Telephone Company chain its directories in the booths?

THOSE "FORBIDDEN" BIBLES

Why does your Church forbid Catholics to read the Bible and at the same time claim that She champions the Bible as the inspired word of God?

You have been misinformed. The Church *encourages* Catholics to read the Bible. The Catholic Church never kept the Bible *from* the people. She kept the Bible *for* the people. The Catholic Church gave the Bible to the world. In the twentieth century, as in the first century, the Catholic Church proclaims the Holy Bible as the Word of God. It was the Catholic Church which determined for the world officially what is the Bible. The Canon or collection of the Sacred Scriptures was both proclaimed and promulgated by her own supreme authority in the general councils of the early Church.

The Catholic Church has ever urged its members to read and cherish it, offers numerous spiritual blessings to those who devoutly read its pages. Priests of the Catholic Church the world over, are obliged to read the Bible every day in reciting the Divine Office composed mainly of the Scriptures.

In the Holy Sacrifice of the Mass daily offered by the priest, the readings are taken from the Bible, and the prayers incorporate many truths taught in the Bible.

THE "BAD CATHOLICS"

What have you got to say about "bad Catholics"? I know a few who are sinful and make a mockery of their religion. They go to church every Sunday, then go right out and commit every sin in the book and make no bones about it. That's one of the main things that I have against the Catholic Church.

Yes, it cannot be denied, there are bad Catholics, crude Catholics, ignorant Catholics; just as there are good Catholics, refined Catholics and intellectual Catholics. Peter's net catches every manner of fish. But look to the doctrine not to the personnel. And never forget that if there are bad Catholics, they are bad not *because of* but *in spite of* the teachings of their Church.

They are bad because they neglect their Catholic duties and thereby disgrace themselves, give scandal to those on the outside, discourage the weak and encourage such as should be restrained. Like fallen angels, they often find new obediences and new zeal in a false cause. But, what about the hundreds of thousands of saintly ones who attend Mass daily before going to work? Our Lord told us not to be scandalized when we see "cockle and wheat" in His Church. The Catholic Church is no more to blame for bad Catholics than a city is to be blamed because criminals live in it.

AND NOW...
...WHAT WILL YOU *DO*?

If one considers well this same unity which Christ implored for His Church, it seems to shine, as it were, with a triple ray of beneficent supernal light: namely, the unity of Catholics among themselves, which must always be kept exemplary and more firm; the unity of prayers and ardent desires with which those Christians separated from this Apostolic See aspire to be united with us; and the unity in esteem and respect for the Catholic Church which animates those who follow non-Christian religions.

> Second Vatican Council: *Opening words of Pope John XXIII*

ON BECOMING A CATHOLIC

I am very strongly inclined to join your Church. What are the conditions that I must fulfill to become a Catholic?

It is very important that you ask yourself why you are inclined. It is possible that you have motives which incline you towards the Catholic religion, yet would not in the least justify you in becoming a Catholic. Do not imagine that I want to discourage you from the Catholic Church. I would do all possible to bring you to it. But if people want to become Catholics they must do so, not on their own terms, but with a full acceptance of all the Church herself demands of us in the name of God.

The Catholic Church requires of all adults who seek admission into her fold, a supernatural sorrow for all past sins and a firm belief in all the teachings of Christ and His Apostles, as handed down from the beginning by the written and unwritten tradition of Christ's one Divine Church. Converts are required to study carefully under the guidance of some priest, an approved catechism, that is, a brief summary of Catholic belief and practice.

One who wants to become a Catholic must first believe wholeheartedly in the Catholic Church and all she teaches. If one has suspicions that she might be wrong on this or that point of dogmatic teaching, it would be a sure sign that such a person had not received the gift of Catholic faith. That person is certainly not in a position to become a Catholic.

Ordinarily, if one can accept these terms, a priest keeps the convert under instructions from three to six months. During this period the convert usually attends Sunday and Holy Day Masses, prays daily and observes the Church laws.

ALBA BOOKS

WELCOME, NUMBER 4,000,000,000! by James V. Schall, S.J. — Christianity has been accused of being the root cause of population and ecology problems. Yet the lesson of history is that the number of men the planet can support is not limited to existing resources: it depends mostly on human creativity which is the supreme resource. As long as there is no limit to human knowledge, there is no effective limit to what knowledge can accomplish.

Fr. Schall treats of politics, environ- and technology in our time, studying each of these in the light of Christian principles. His book will be welcomed by the intelligent reader dissatisfied with conventional wisdom, and it will be found especially useful by students of these problems.

145 — ISBN O — 8189 — 114 $1.75

WORKING WITH PARISH COUNCILS? by William J. Rademacher — Fr. Rademacher brings together here, under handy headings, the most frequently recurring questions and answers from his monthly feature in TODAY'S PARISH magazine.

Perennial parish council problems are extensively treated: Pastors, Members, Proper and Fair Procedure, Liturgy, Women in the Church and many others. There are also two splendid chapters on the whole theory of Church and Parish and on the relationship between different ministries. The pastoral wisdom and expertise of Fr. Rademacher are always very much in evidence.

This is the ideal quick-reference work for people in parish ministry who, faced with a new problem, don't know where to turn. $1.75

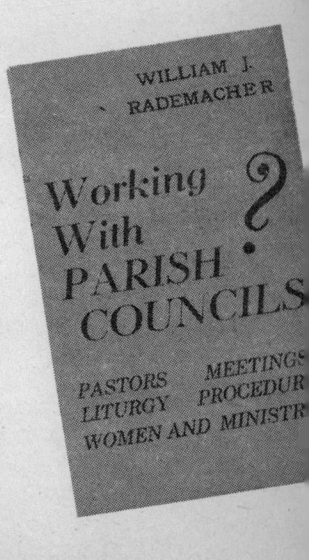

SEXUALITY SUMMARY by William J. Allen, J.C.D. — After all the debate and discussion of the past ten years, how much do people really KNOW about sexual morality? Have there been any new developments? How do you "form your conscience"? Has the "anything goes" principle become respectable?

Here is a clear, coherent, convincing and compassionate picture of four main problem areas: homosexuality, abortion, contraception and premarital sex. It outlines the best modern thinking in these areas and the solutions proposed. Fully updated and complete with extensive Bibliography for further reading, it is the most practical work on this subject to appear in many years.

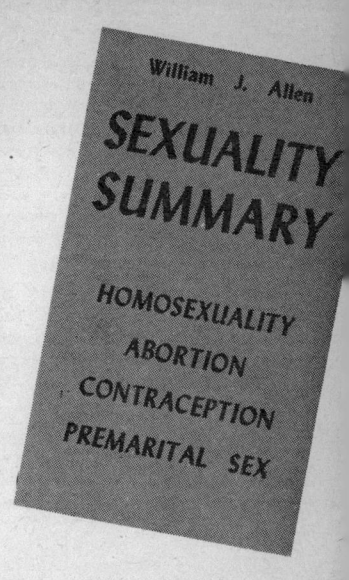

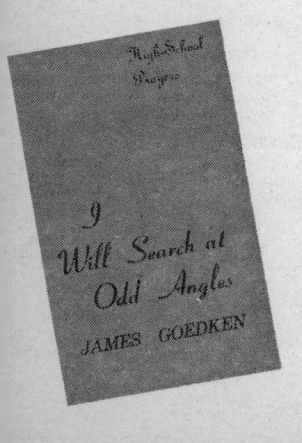

$1.75

I SEARCH AT ODD ANGLES by James Goedken — Books of prayer are available, but how many of them have been written with High School students in mind?

This one has. It is immersed in life and speaks of life. These Scripture-based prayers have been formulated for his students by Fr. Goedken day by day over several years.

Divided into Themes like Thanking, Loving, Wondering, Listening, Believing and many others, this book of prayers will be found just right for School Assemblies, Youth Groups, Prayer Groups and, not least, for family prayer.

$1.75

THE MARIJUANA MAZE by Harold J. Pascal, C.M. — Marijuana has been known for at least a thousand years but never before has it been so widely used and never before has its use generated so much controversy. The opposing sides in the debate are well-armed with statistics, and contradictory research results have produced what the author of this informative volume rightly calls a "maze."

His purpose is to indicate a way out of this confusion. In crisp, non-technical language he reduces the question to understandable terms, supporting his statements with accurate and up-to-date figures.

The book is essential reading for parents, educators and for everyone preoccupied by the sight of so many young people taking the path to possible self-destruction. $1.75

GROWING OLD GRACEFULLY by J. Maurus — Before the end of the century millions in this country will have to face the problem of growing old. Yet, age is not just something marked on the calendar; it is something marked on the character. In the phrase "growing old," the operative word is "growing." Even on the threshold of eternity we can still progress as persons.

GROWING OLD GRACEFULLY handles the many problems of old age with understanding, intelligence and constructive skill. It is a highly-practical and well planned book, an ideal guide to happy closing years.

— $1.75

Are there ALBA BOOKS titles you want but cannot find in your local stores? Simply send name of book and retail price plus 30¢ to cover mailing and handling costs to:
ALBA BOOKS, Canfield, Ohio, 44406.